Lockdown or Economic Destruction?

Madan Sabnavis

Published by

PUBLISHERS & DISTRIBUTORS (P) LTD
7/22, Ansari Road, Darya Ganj, New Delhi-110002
Phones : +91-11-40775252, 40775214, 23273880, 23275880
Fax: +91-11-23285873
Web: www.atlanticbooks.com
E-mail: orders@atlanticbooks.com

Disclaimer

- The author and the publisher have taken every effort to the maximum of their skill, expertise and knowledge to provide correct material in the book. Even then if some mistakes persist in the content of the book, the publisher does not take responsibility for the same. The publisher shall have no liability to any person or entity with respect to any loss or damage caused, or alleged to have been caused directly or indirectly, by the information contained in this book.
- The author has fully tried to follow the copyright law. However, if any work is found to be similar, it is unintentional and the same should not be used as defamatory or to file legal suit against the author.
- If the readers find any mistakes, we shall be grateful to them for pointing out those to us so that these can be corrected in the next edition.
- All disputes are subject to the jurisdiction of Delhi courts only.

Printed & bound in India by Atlantic Print Services

For Charu and Ragini

Acknowledgements

This book would not have been possible without being able to access the ground level stories and views of various institutions and organizations since April 2020. All the data-based facts that have been presented here owe their utterance to these sources which add weight to the arguments provided here, which would otherwise have been plain opinion.

This book has been written almost on a continuous basis for around 9-10 months as the issue of lockdown and its travails were felt the moment it was announced. While there was a lot of suffering during the period, I thought it best to examine these issues and collate the subjects on an ongoing basis so that there could be a coherent analysis of the same. Careful reading of a number of online publications on a daily basis provided substance to my thoughts and it is not possible to acknowledge all these sources individually.

I would like to thank the editors of various newspapers for publishing various pieces on the pandemic which I had written which ensured that I was abreast with all the developments and able to present analysis regularly. In particular, I would like to thank the late Sunil Jain (Managing Editor of Financial Express) and Sarthak Ray for carrying virtually a weekly article which commented on various aspects of the lockdown. I am also grateful to Puneet Wadhwa (Business Standard for taking my instant reactions on each and every policy announcement), A. Srinivas and J. Srinivasan (Business Line), and R.N. Bhaskar (Free Press Journal) for publishing my articles. While the essays in this book have been independently written with detailed analysis, commenting on contemporary developments helped me to develop a clearer perspective which hopefully has been manifested in this book.

This book has been inspired as usual by my wife Charu, who has provided the direction to me right from the time we studied together in Delhi School of Economics and my daughter Ragini whose continuous discussions at the dining table helped in strengthening my thinking. Continuous discussions with my brother Madhukar and sister-in law Farida also helped in sharpening the ideas over time.

I am also thankful to my parents—my father, late S.R.K. Rao, an eminent economist who in a way was also a victim of covid, as no hospital was willing to admit a non-covid patient who was 90 years of age, and my mother Kamala.

Finally, I would like to thank Harjeet Singh and the entire team at Atlantic Publishers and Distributors Pvt. Ltd. for their effort in converting this manuscript to a book. This has been done in a very timely manner notwithstanding the lockdowns and other restrictions.

Madan Sabnavis

Prologue

Bandra Bandstand is a well-known place in Mumbai which has all the glamour that one can ask for. There are residences of some Bollywood stars in the vicinity, and the buildings around house some of the most affluent individuals. The little promenade that separates the sea from the mainland is a good place for walking and has been well developed to make it walkable. In the morning and evening one can see several people taking a walk or jog from as early as 5 before sunrise. The place is quite good for such activities with some exercise poles in corners. At the same time, it is not too large to monitor. And yes, there are security personnel around who make sure that people don't bring their bikes on the path or litter the pathway.

It is also a leveler in the sense that it is open to all and hence even the plebeian gentry can walk in and take their strolls or loiter around. The pathway to the sea is rocky and one can see groups of people just walking over these rocks which can stretch for over 200 metres when there is a low tide. Some of the poorer sections find puddles of water to bathe or wash their clothes while the youngster couples use this romantic setting for being together squatting on the rocks. There is also a regular middle class which is there that come in their vehicles and then take a stroll before it becomes too late when the cops could fine them for wrongful parking.

Thus, this promenade cuts across classes and there is perfect harmony with no one getting in the way of others. One can see some politicians also walking along in groups with followers ever keen to hear what they have to say. It is an ideal setting for a city which cuts across religion, class, and caste.

It is mid-December2020 and the round 5 of 'Unlock' is well on the way. There are boards at the start of lanes which lead to the promenade indicating that it is meant for only residents. There are no guards there which means that there was time when the Mount Mary Hill had containment buildings which no longer holds. The authorities are probably just too tired to take these boards away as this has been going on for just too long a time. There is another commonality among the walkers or squatters there.

Very few find it necessary to use masks and walking around gives one the feeling that this could have been in 2019 rather than 2020. The 80-20 rules hold in the wrong direction as there are more without masks than those with. And another 50% of the 20% have their masks down and hence show tokenism when it comes to wearing masks. This is a full 8 months since the lockdown was announced.

People appear to think that it is back to normal now that the lockdown has been eased. Or, there is a cavalier attitude that nothing will happen. Or, may there be fatigue built over time which manifests in this indifference. And often there is a demonstration effect that if we see people not using masks, we follow suit.

The interesting thing was that there were two sets of policemen at two different spots in groups of three. While they had their masks on, they were least bothered in fining or even asking the people to use masks. It was a clear case of indifference or fatigue which pervaded the environment.

This background tells everything about the way people in India look at the lockdown and the epidemic eight months after the economy was subjected to a panic exercise. This scene could be replayed anywhere else in the world. The fact that both the educated and not so educated behave in the same way is important as it is human behaviour which comes into play. This is human behaviour after going through a record number of 10 million victims of the virus and over one lakh deaths.

If this is how our response has been, the fair question to ask is whether we did really think that having a lockdown for 21 days would have actually delivered the impossible result of keeping everyone at home to ensure that the infection did not spread? The extended lockdown, hence, was a disaster to begin with and the economy was struggling to get back on its feet till December.

There are awkward questions raised when the unlock started. How can the government open the economy when the number of daily cases was rising exponentially from a few thousands to 50,000 and then to over 90,000? Quite clearly the government had lost the plot and just like the imposition was a desperate measure so was the unlock which had to be done under severe contradictions in the state of spread of virus.

The lockdown globally was a man-made disaster. Countries have recovered at different paces depending on how quickly the governments have relaxed the rules. Most developed countries did so when the number of infections came down. However, India had to do so when they were rising. The western countries now recognize that even as the second wave hit the shores, lockdown was not the answer and, hence, the economic repercussions would be less severe. As can be seen as we entered the seventh month, the IMF has reported improved forecast for several countries. Prima facie this is one crisis where countries can recover faster because it is a man-made event. There are no collapses in the financial sector as was the case with Lehman, Asian crisis, stock market, or S&L. Therefore, there is hope. There is need for affirmative action to be taken by all governments to hasten the recovery process and this is a tough call as seen in our case. But, still one can never be sure that the virus is behind us even after the population is vaccinated.

The foregoing essays would talk on various issues which came up during the lockdown and the unlocking process which caused considerable damage to the economy and more importantly the morale of the common man. While all nations move on and this episode will be forgotten as being another aberration, there would be millions of people whose lives have turned upside down much like what happens when there is a natural disaster.

Admittedly, several measures have been taken to alleviate the suffering. But, were they adequate or just too conservative? Could the government have done more? It is left to the reader to decide if this was inevitable or necessary or just another blunder.

At the end of the day, we will forget this event which will go down in history as just another shock to which the 'resilient' citizens came out quite well. It happens when there are riots where several people die, or earthquakes or cyclones. The fatalistic nature of Indians ensures that this resilience comes in. Even for man-made catastrophes like demonetization, few remember the travails and, hence, is a positive reflection of society at large. We tend to be too positive or keep conveying the gains made from any such decision to the extent that the negatives don't enter the frame. The information technology shoulder is used even here as it has been interpreted as having revolutionized the way we work and live just like how the travails of demonetization were outshouted by the gains of digitization. Similarly, this episode too will be forgotten once it is behind us. In fact, since October the talk of the vaccine has made one almost forget the series of challenges that the citizens had gone through, and the talk has moved from lockdown to the implementation of the immunization programme.

List of Abbreviations

ACMA	Automotive Components Manufacturers Association
ADB	Asian Development Bank
ADSCR	Average debt service coverage ratio
AN	Atma Nirbhar
CAG	Comptroller and Auditor General of India
CAIT	Confederation of All India Traders
CBI	Central Bureau of Investigation
CCD	Café Coffee Day
CEO	Chief Executive Officer
CICs	Credit Information companies
CMIE	Centre for Monitoring Indian Economy
CRR	Cash reserve ratio
CSO	Central Statistics Office
CTC	Cost to company
CVC	Central Vigilance Commission
DISCOM	Distribution company (power)
DSCR	Debt service coverage ratio
EBIDTA	Earnings before interest, depreciation, taxes and amortization
ECLGS	Emergency credit line guarantee scheme
EPF	Employee Provident Fund
F&B	Food & beverages
FI	Financial Institution
FMCG	Fast moving consumer good

FRBM	Fiscal responsibility and budget management
GeM	Government e Marketplace
GST	Goods and services tax
HFC	Housing Finance Company
HT	Hindustan Times
ILO	International Labour Organization
IMF	International Monetary Fund
IT	Information technology
KCC	Kisan Credit Card
LAF	Liquidity Adjustment Facility
LTC	Leave travel concession
LTRO	Long term repo operation
MFI	Micro finance institution
MFNREGA	Mahatma Gandhi National Rural Employee Guarantee Act
MSF	Marginal Standing Facility
MSME	Micro, small and medium enterprises
NABARD	National Bank for Agriculture and Rural Development
NBFC	Non-Bank finance company
NCGTC	National Credit Guarantee Trustee Company
NGO	Non-Government Organization
NHB	National Housing Bank
NSSF	National Small Savings Fund
OMC	Oil Marketing companies
OMO	Open Market Operations
OTR	One time restructuring
PDS	Public Distribution System
PF	Provident Fund
PFC	Power Finance Corporation
PLI	Performance Linked Incentive

PMGKP	Pm Garib Kalyan Package
PMI	Purchasing Managers' Index
PMMY	PM MUDRA Yojana
PSBs	Public sector banks
PTI	Pres Trust of India
QE	Quantitative easing
RAI	Retailers Association of India
RERA	Real Estate Regulation Authority
RP	Resolution Plan
SIDBI	Small Industries Development Bank of India
SMA	Special mention Account
SME	Small and Medium Enterprise
SOP	Standard Operating Practice
Tbill	Treasury Bill
TLTRO	Targeted Long term repo operation
TNW	Tangible net worth
TOL	Total outstanding liabilities
UN	United Nations
WFH	Work From Home
WMA	Ways and Means Advances
WTO	World Trade Organization

Contents

Acknowledgements .... *v*
Prologue .... *vii*
List of Abbreviations .... *xi*
Introduction .... *xvii*

EXPERIENCES

1. Micro Woes: What you went Through 3
2. Ground Level Revelations 9
3. Migrants 17
4. Periodic Lockdowns 30
5. The Unlock Mystery 38

MACROECONOMIC EFFECTS

6. GDP—The First Casualty 45
7. Job Destruction 58
8. SME Saga of Never-Ending Woes 68
9. Investment Collapses 76
10. PMI Dithers 80
11. Inflation Rises 84
12. Corporate Performance: Strange Signals 90
13. Fiscal Balances get Hurt without Giving Anything 94
14. The GST Farce 103

POLICY APPROACH

15. The Grand Design or an Apology for Stimulus ... 111
16. What have Other Countries Done?...................... 129
17. The RBI Response 140
(a) The Liquidity Deluge..................................... 140
(b) Bank Moratorium 147
(c) Emergency Line of Credit............................... 153
(d) One-time Restructuring.................................. 156

RUMINATIONS

18. Industries that must Reinvent 167
19. Epilogue... 179
20. Your Judgement.. 186
References.. 194
Index 196

Introduction

Demonetization was probably one of the biggest economic shocks imposed by the government on the country which caused substantial disruption in everyday life. The goal was to try and get rid of black money and control the spread of counterfeit currency. At a later stage, the objective turned to making people go digital; but to argue that the entire country is sent scurrying to change currency to get into the habit of using digital currency is disingenuous to say the least. However, as people underwent enormous hardship and economic activity came to a standstill for almost 5 months, the data on economic growth was a bigger shock as the CSO vouched that the economy did very well and grew by 8.1%—which was one of the highest rates achieved in the new GDP series, i.e., from FY13 onwards. The defenders of demonetization still argue that black money has been curtailed though there is no data to support the same. This is important because in India we rarely accept policy mistakes and normally tend to convince the masses with high decibel pitches on how successful the initiatives were. Hence, even for the lockdown notwithstanding the severe hardship that the entire country had to bear, there would be a large contingent of intelligentsia which will tend to over-praise the measures taken.

The shutdown or lockdown as it came to be called would probably the first and largest man-made economic crises across the world and while the imposition of the same in March 2020 could not have been challenged as the whole world went in for the same, the consequences of such a move have been dire in our context. It will be hard for policy makers to admit that it was a mistake and the supposition that if it were not done, the spread of infection would have been greater, cannot be contested as it is hypothetical. But, two months into the shutdown, the decision was taken to roll back the lockdown in hesitant phases. The curious factor was that spread of the virus had accelerated and while the world has seen the peaking and subsequent plateauing of the incidence, in the Indian case it was still in the upward stage in the month of June. Therefore, to say that a shutdown helps in stopping the spread of the virus cannot be justified in our context.

To put the severity of the covid pandemic in some perspective, as of January 2021, there were over 100 million cases across the world and the number of deaths crossed 2 million. In 2019, as per the WHO, 8.9 million people died due to heart ailments, 6.2 million due to stroke, 3.2 million due to pulmonary related diseases, 2.6 million from lower respiratory ailments, and 2 million in the neonatal category. While the number of infections is scary, the fatality rate at 2 million is probably on par with some of the other diseases in the world but, much lower than the heart related ailments. But, coming as it did in the form of a pandemic, the fear of the unknown, caused considerable panic leading to herd mentality in terms of reaction, lockdown appeared to be logical.

What was the logic behind the lockdown? Evidently, the socio-economic factors play a role in validating this theory. When people stay in proximity and space is at a premium which is a case in metropolitan India where slums dominate the landscape, social distancing is not possible. Therefore, the logical argument was that people locked up for 14 days would be detected, treated, and cured of the virus. Hence, the possibility of the virus spreading was to be low. But, this was not the case in India.

A pertinent question raised at the beginning was: what are we waiting for? Some argued that it was the flattening of the curve. But, as the number of tests conducted started increasing, the number of cases being detected started rising. As the sordid drama of tackling migrants was finally taken up at a humanistic level, the spread of the virus to the interiors ensued. Therefore, no one knew what flattening meant as the curve was only increasing.

As people moved and more people were tested, there would be the tendency for the numbers to increase.

The consequence of this 'jugaad' approach to the lockdown was that economic activity was impacted sharply. Output fell, factories closed down, services came to a standstill, unemployment increased, people were living with less income and with uncertainty; and for all practical purposes it was a race on a daily basis to procure provisions to run the households as goods disappeared from the stores. Prices of food items increased even though the Ministry of Agriculture claimed that the Rabi production was at a high. Supply chains got disrupted and chaos reigned.

The Immediate Response

There was the touch of the dramatic which appeals to Indians just like any 'tamasha' on the roadside when the traffic stops leading to congestions when there is an accident. People were asked to bang utensils together at the appointed time and while there are no recorded numbers, the cacophony was immense. Did we really think that this noise would scare the virus was the questions asked by cynics especially in this age of science and technology? Others defended such an action as being symbolic which fostered unity among the masses that was required before the big announcement was made on the lockdown. A couple of weeks later the nation was asked to put off lights and light candles or lamps in unison and while this was less dramatic and more sober, the nation obliged. But, when it came to staying indoors for three weeks, it was difficult to comply, and it was only after the process started did the serious obstacles come to light.

We evidently like the dramatic but are not willing to be disciplined as the latter is a continued action. A common-sense driven principle is that if everyone outside their homes uses a mask to cover the mouth and nose, the spreading of the virus diminishes significantly, and society is better off. But, this never happens not just in India but in all countries, which have witnessed high infection numbers.

Federalism Spoils the Show

The enthusiasm with which the lockdown was imposed by the centre and supported by the states was immense. However, the contradictions of a federal set up came into play at every stage with every state having its own rules and concerns. Therefore, while the centre allowed some activity like say courier services, the same was not allowed across states. While goods could be transported if they were essentials, the same were stopped and drivers beaten up by the police across the border. This had made the situation quite chaotic at the ground level. The national level lockdown imposed in March exposed the rather ruthless and insensitive nature of the police force which went by the book and beat up anyone on the road who did not satisfy them with a reason for being out. Hence, migrants who were out of work and money and walked their way back to their distant homes had to face the ignominy of being beaten by the police along the way with no sympathy being shown until such time that the centre announced a plan to take them back home.

What is certain is that the government was unable to conjecture the road to be taken as the spread of the epidemic till July was phenomenal. With the economy in disarray there were few attempts made to draw up an economic roadmap and the federalism in the country had literally meant that one step ahead taken by the centre has been accompanied by three steps back by several states. Hence, as far as economic players are concerned there was no certainty about the future. While business is ready to follow SOPs (standard operating procedures) to ensure that the wheels move, imposition of randomized lockdowns by various authorities including states, municipals, and panchayats has meant that the only certainty in the economy with regards to policy is 'uncertainty'. This is always unsettling for business.

The curious part of the selective lockdowns that have been imposed is that they follow the same route taken in March. There was only hope that things would settle down in 14 days and if that did not materialize the solution was to extend the same for another 14 days. Also, there have been no relief measures provided anywhere when there are localized lockdowns and unlike the national level one where the centre provided an array of relief measures, states have been quite untouched with the human aspect and have brought in these temporary lockdowns with an iron fist and no accompanying relief. Quite clearly, the direction of the lockdown got diluted along the way.

Government Steps in with Relief

The government has tried to placate feelings by announcing economic packages which along with the RBI measures were to deliver relief. But, is it enough? Will they really help? Why not transfer ₹ 1 lakh into account of every family like has been done in the west? There are arguments on both sides and the decision of the government was more aligned to enable relief rather than give the same through the budget. What was given was in a limited manner and as the unlocking started, got diluted significantly or were just terminated. It was assumed that people would fend for themselves. Similarly, the RBI opened the taps of liquidity in different forms, but the fundamental question raised was whether will anyone borrow money if they are not allowed to produce a good or service?

It does appear that the lockdown was announced in a hurry and there was a sense of panic. Opposing this at that time would have meant being labelled as a dissonant and, hence, there was acceptance that the plan was the best. However, three months down the line there did not seem to be any firm plan; and the easiest way to overcome the question on what to do when the period of shutdown was coming to an end was to extend the same. This was done five times and while the centre announced some relaxation the states had their viewpoint and, hence, added to the confusion.

The Final Impact

Against this background, this book tries to evaluate the economic damage caused by the lockdown which in a way was man-made as it was a conscious policy decision taken at that time. The premise is that this decision was taken without really having in place a plan and the boat was in a way rudderless and moved with the tide with the oar being used at times to keep the barge floating. Neither the direction nor the course was known, and it was a case of living on hope that the flattening of the curve would take place. At some point it was realized that the spread could not be stopped by a lockdown as the establishment could not take care of the requirements of the population by providing an income as well as supply of goods and services. The partial relaxation followed with a plethora of notifications added to the chaos.

The reason to be critical of the entire approach is that the lockdown per se did not quite help to stop the spread; and ex-post one could say that the high density of population in urban India makes sitting at home near impossible. Also, with the administrative machinery being weak, it was not possible to actually provide the citizens with their daily necessities so as to ensure that no one stepped out and spread the virus. Further when it comes to 'slum India', the living conditions are so abysmal which we have accepted for some many decades that trying to change living in three weeks was ridiculous. Dharavi (a large slum in Mumbai) which was a hotbed for the virus has 225 community toilets for a population density of 2.27 lakh per sq km which means that there are thousands of people thronging to these spots in the morning at virtually the same time.

By the time it was realized that the economy was sinking fast as goods disappeared from the market and more people entered the stream of not having enough money to live, the government began rolling back the constraints put on economic activity and the lockdowns with suffixes of 2, 3, 4, 5, and 6 became more liberal. But, this was also the time when the number of cases in India progressively increased and the so-called flattening which was spoken was never really witnessed as the numbers touched almost a lakh and came down suddenly by Diwali ostensibly due to a lower number of tests that were conducted and then rose almost immediately. There never seemed to be a pattern anyway. Also, given the western experiences, the onset of the second wave means that no one really knew if things were settling down or would ever normalize before another round of infection started.

So, we had a situation where India was opening as the number of infections spread fast while the story was in reverse in other countries which had already seen their worst and were witnessing the declining slope in incremental cases. As of June-end India was probably the second most infected country and, in a way, helpless in the economic sense even while the excellent approach of the health machinery addressed the issue of cure and kept the incidence of death low at around 3% of infected patients which was commendable as other nations had higher rates.

The result of the damage will never be known as it will stretch for at least a couple of years during which time there could be several other developments. In fact, as the economy unlocked and economic activity commenced, economic numbers started looking better and this was used to prove that the economy was back on the recovery path. By early 2021, there were very loud decibel levels claiming that the economy was back on track and that we were over the hill. Time is of essence because after any crisis economies revert to the average as nothing is stagnant. Merely because the economy reaches normalcy after a point of time does not wipe out the damage caused as there are people involved whose livelihoods have been affected.

The book looks at various economic facets that have been distorted due to the lockdown and does some crystal ball gazing of what the future will look like with this new experience of working from home amid panic and fear as no one knows if the pandemic will return even if it seems to end. The approach is dispassionate and objective, and places as many facts that are available to the reader. These facts are not interpretations that have been taken from published sources and, hence, are not biased views. These are micro views which cannot be generalized but give a flavour of what had happened in different areas.

The second part is macro-economic data analysis of data which got distorted by the lockdown. Here variables like investment, GDP, inflation, etc. are analyzed while being blended with the micro analysis at some places. Hence, when we talk of employment, the reader is presented with what the press reported on different professions along with what some surveys found. This is then blended with corporate data on financial performance to provide a complete picture. It is felt that this approach will drive home the point well.

There is also a section on what all was done by the government to control the ill effects of the lockdown, and this is something that has to be appreciated because the intervention was quite immediate. This gives credit to the government. However, was it enough? That is a moot point as we draw examples of what other countries have done to alleviate the situation. The reader may feel that more could have been done.

Finally, there is an open debate which has been presented. Was the lockdown the right thing or rather the only solution? The author's view is that it was an error, and not well planned. While it can be justified on grounds of something that needs to be done, it would take courage to admit that it was an error or judgment. But, the arguments are put on both sides so that the readers can decide for themselves which side of the line they are on. There are definitely no clear answers as the consequences of not doing it is a matter of conjecture that will never be known.

Experiences

Chapter 1

Micro Woes: What you went Through

And no one showed us to the land
And no one knows the where's or why's

—Pink Floyd: Echoes

The lockdown that was announced affected each and every person in the country. The rules laid down were straight forward. One was not allowed to leave their homes and could do so only for purchasing essential goods. The definition of essential goods was quite nebulous, and the local authority decided on the same. What could be delivered to the homes was milk. But here too the delivery chains were stopped across borders which meant that it was not certain if you could get milk at the regular time. Several milk dealers complained that their trucks could not cross the borders of states and districts due to differential interpretation of the curfew rules which led to rotting of the produce which meant substantial monetary loss. This played out across all States.

Printing of newspapers were permitted by the central government but the local authorities came in the way and did not allow circulation. Printing presses closed and could not operate. This was notwithstanding the fact that the PM had made it clear that newspapers did not carry the risk of carrying the virus and was a part of the essential goods. You had to get news from the Internet or TV channels. Even when the printing of papers began in an anemic form, individuals were not allowed to get their copies as the respective societies had them on the forbidden list.

Fruits and vegetables were permitted to be sold. There were fixed timings and these restrictions meant that one had to hurry to the nearest shop and pick up these products. The vendors had a problem getting their supplies, and as the main mandis were closed had to use other channels for procurement. To begin with the identification of any one in the mandi with the virus meant close down for periods of two-seven days which meant supplies were distorted and the farmers as well as traders were hit hard. Not surprisingly, prices rose sharply. Two hours in the morning was permitted and if one were lucky, could find some vendors in the evening. The supplies were disrupted in most cases as the logistics support was not available and hence even excess supplies at the farm gate translated into higher prices due to the inability of the vendors to pick up their produce.

Regular *kirana* stores were open but could sell only essentials. At times, the police would beat up and closed down the shop if shampoo was being sold as it was not considered an essential good. These shops had restricted timings too depending on the whims of the local authority.

To begin with the identification of a single patient in a housing society led to the entire complex being declared a covid zone and hence Section 144 became more draconian. The entire geography was divided into red, orange, and green zones for this purpose. Ironically, as the number of red zones increased with more complexes being called covid-affected zones, it became a logistical hurdle to monitor the same. Subsequently, the local authority defined the number of cases that would classify the complex or building into a covid zone. By the end of the year, the rules were relaxed significantly with a step-down approach. From the single building in a complex being notified it was diluted to the floor concerned and finally to the individual house where there was a single patient. Fatigue was the overriding factor in diluting the intensity of monitoring of these zones.

The trauma of the covid patient was immense. Any covid case reported would mean the entire family being tested as well as the people that were in touch with the family. The Aarogya Setu tool which monitored the same once a person had it installed on their phone turned into a nightmare as contact tracing started. The rather inhuman treatment of families was manifested in the local authorities sending various family members to different hospitals in the town/city which added to the trauma of those already housing a covid patient. Infected persons often had to bribe the authority to ensure that all were sent to the same hospital. Further, even if patients were asymptomatic, they were forced to be quarantined in the hospital to begin with and the cost of treatment could range from a few thousands in a public centre to ₹ 15-20 lakhs in high-end hospitals as there was forced stay for 14 days. The monetary burden suffered by families was immense. There was no way of contesting these costs as hospitals became exploitative and there was no check put by the authorities.

Things became better when people were given the option of self-quarantining in their homes with only those who were serious being compelled to go to the hospital. But on the whole, there was a fear factor of taking a test because if found to be infected even if asymptomatic, there was a possibility of harassment as there were no uniform laws being followed across the country.

The curfew rules made it clear that between nine in the night and six in the morning no one could be seen on the road, and action could be taken if found outside. One had to shop within a vicinity of four kms or even less. If found driving and asked the reason, one could be arrested if there was no satisfactory answer. As expected, the rich in cars could get away, but the poor were often caned for being on the road.

The problem in a place like Mumbai was acute. Several habitations have people living in shifts in little double-storied rooms and with a loss of job had to stay huddled in the same room. Under normal circumstances half the inhabitants would stay in the room for half a day while the others went for work. In the second shift, it would be the other way round. With the lockdown all were forced to stay in the same habitat which under summer conditions became challenging. This led to not just the spread of infection but also forced movement on the roads which led in turn to the police taking action. The problem was compounded by the fact that it was mid-summer where it was not possible for 10 people or more to reside in a room of 100 square feet the whole day. With all transport coming to a halt these people could not go to their villages and were stuck at home with no income to support them.

But even the rich could not get away easily. All housing complexes were locked, and people could not move out when they wanted. Police vans patrolling would check up registers kept at the gates to see who came and went. Any trespass could be met with a fine or even a threat of imprisonment as Section 144 was imposed which was quite extraordinary as it is normally done to ensure there are no violent actions on the part of the public. Nobody was aware of what the curfew laws stated and how they were interpreted leading to considerable acrimony and dissonance among people.

Public transport came to a halt and those functioning could only ferry workers who came under essential services. Hence, if one did not have the right identity card, entry on buses was forbidden. The anomaly was stark as those belonging to public sector banks could use public transport while those in private banks could not. This was even though banking was classified as an essential service and covered both the sectors. This was reversed much later when the private sector bankers were also allowed to travel. As of January 2021, the Mumbai local trains were open only to public sector employees of essential services. The resumption of services for all from February 1st had a caveat where only essential services personnel could travel through the day and the non-essential had to move out of the station before seven in the morning. This was hardly helpful.

Rules were nebulous for doctors who were not given flexibility in working. In some places, they were not allowed to operate their clinics while in others there were fixed timings. Home visits were possible but that cost the patients more money. Any illness at home particularly for children and senior citizens meant more challenges at home. While some doctors could be consulted through the online mode if not available at the clinics, this was not the general practice. Therefore, the rule of law as well as the fear of catching infection came in the way of finding a medical solution for ailments. Not surprisingly, fewer patients of non-covid disease were reported.

During the first phase of the lockdown which started in March and went on till June when the unlock started, hospitals were closed for all non-covid cases, and it was hard to get treatment for regular ailments. Almost all hospitals became covid zones and the fear of infection ensured that other patients were excluded from getting any treatment. This caused a lot of distress to the diseased section which included several senior citizens. Those requiring surgeries or treatment of other ailments related to heart, kidney, liver, etc. had to defer their visits as the hospitals were closed for them.

There were different rules put on getting in domestic help at home. To begin with there was a blanket ban of all movement which meant that this category could not go for work under curfew laws. This held for the first three months everywhere. Subsequently, it was realized that this class was not being paid salaries just like organized labour when companies were forced to stop production. This prompted the local governments to give explicit permission to allow domestic help to be allowed to work and societies which objected could be penalized. Normalcy started from August onwards albeit in a limited manner as the decision was left to individuals rather than societies.

The resumption of non-essential services from July onwards (though signals were given in some places earlier) was the first positive move for some of them which enabled them to claw their way back towards normalcy. Yet services like gymnasiums, hotels, restaurants, travel agencies were virtually blocked well into the New Year. In Mumbai, from November onwards restaurants could be kept open for diners with several restrictions. However, their staff could not come for work as this class was part of the migrant labour or stayed in places which were accessible by local trains which were out of bounds. Therefore, operations were minimal for those which worked, while around 30-50% remained closed.

These images would hold for any reader as they were universal in India. Even during war times which goes back to the early seventies, there were never such restrictions imposed on people and the system became virtually clueless on the future steps. The uncertainty was unnerving for everyone and the absence of announcements from the top ceased by May and post June it was left to States and district authorities to have their own plans of opening which was not in consonance with that of the Centre. In a way, it appeared that the Central Government had said—from now on each authority would have their own plans. As every State or authority worked on its jurisdiction there was no harmony in action across them leading to even greater uncertainty and often, chaos.

By February 2021, the dust had almost settled as activities across were moving somewhere near normal, albeit in a hesitant manner as different towns and cities followed their SOPs. The general restrictions and definition of containment areas remained with any increase in the infection cases being met with some regression to the past. The positive development however was the discovery of a vaccine where the challenge was on administering the same. This provided the necessary diversion as citizens discussed when their turn would come and whether the vaccine would be available in the private market.

Chapter 2
Ground Level Revelations

Now I've got that feeling once again
I can't explain you would not understand
This is not how I am
I have become comfortably numb

—Pink Floyd: Comfortably numb

Admittedly, the ground level situation had been evolving and after six months of the lockdown things looked better and more assuring than they did in the initial few months. In fact, in December, it did seem that the country looked more normal than before though not yet at the pre-covid levels. Therefore, often we do tend to look over the travails that the nation went through with the lockdown being in place all through the country. Here we try to capture some of the revelations based on media reports at different points of time ever since the lockdown was announced in the last week of March. These numbers may or may not have been realized finally as these were thoughts expressed by industry which held firmly in the first two months when the lockdown was total. They were quick calculations based on what appeared to have been the cost in the immediate run given the seasonal factors which drive most businesses.

When the lockdown was announced in March, ACMA (Automotive Components Manufacturers of India) had stated that due to 21-day nationwide lockdown in the wake of coronavirus outbreak, the domestic auto component industry was suffering a loss of around ₹ 1,200 crore per day. Intuitively, this would mean a loss of around ₹ 25,000 crore.

On April 20, a big player in the heavy appliances industry said that it will be impacted by a significant loss of up to 60% in March and almost 100% in April. These two months put together contributed to close to 25% of the annual revenue.

On 3rd May the *Telegraph* reported that the consumer durable industry expects a 30% decline in business on account of the lockdown affecting sales in the first quarter. A recovery in the second half of the fiscal would depend on the demand and liquidity conditions of both individuals and industry. The consumer appliances industry is estimated to be valued at around ₹ 75,000 crore, of which around 80% comes from air-conditioners, refrigerators, coolers and freezers. Sales of these items in the first quarter comprise 36% of the total sales, driven by the seasonal summer demand.

The Consumer Electronics and Appliances Manufacturers Association argued that April was a total washout and that a large part of the sales in May would also be impacted on account of the restrictions. Even if things started to open up it was believed that the local authorities may not allow full-fledged operations. June sales would also not be normal. Therefore, the association had projected that the industry would degrow by around 30%. The IIP growth number for computers, electronics, and optical products was – 64%!

Azim Premji University had carried out a survey of nearly 5,000 self-employed, casual, and regular wage workers across 12 States of India between 13 April and 23 May in collaboration with civil society organisations. The survey found a massive increase in unemployment and an equally dramatic fall in earnings. Two-thirds of the respondents had lost work. The few informal workers who were still employed during the lockdown saw their earnings drop by more than half.

Interestingly, contrary to the commonly held belief that agriculture was insulated from the lockdown, an overwhelming majority of farmers could not sell their produce or had to sell at lower prices. It is necessary to understand the harm caused mainly due to poor communication from above. The agricultural sector was formally excluded from the lockdown but once access to mandis was restricted due to the absence of transport facilities as well as fewer traders in the market, the ability to sell got affected.

Casual and self-employed workers were the worst impacted. About half of the wage workers received no salary or reduced salary during the lockdown which was expected. Further, almost eight in 10 people were eating less food than before which also shows that while the government scheme of providing food for the poor was well intended, there were loopholes at the implementation level in various states. Further, more than six of every 10 respondents in urban areas did not have enough money for a week's worth of essentials. Not surprisingly, more than a third of all respondents had taken a loan to cover expenses during the lockdown. Also, around eight in 10 respondents did not have money to pay next month's rent.

The other revelation from the survey was that the direct public spending was not in proportion to the severity of the situation at the ground level, since the bulk of the stimulus package focused on increasing liquidity rather than direct spending. Even the announced relief measures, inadequate as they were, had not reached large sections of the economically vulnerable population. Only a third of the respondents received the Jan Dhan cash transfer. Half of their respondents reported not receiving any cash transfers. This is significant because often one gets to read about the headline announcements made and never really get to know how these schemes are implemented and whether the beneficiaries get what is promised.

According to Confederation of All India Traders (CAIT), Survey as of July 20, the pandemic had caused a loss of ₹ 16 lakh crore to the retail sector. Also, even after Unlock-I traders were still concerned about minimum footfalls due to restrictions on movement of people and absence of workers due to large scale migration. It estimated that such a situation had potential of causing shutdown of 20% of shops in the absence of these rules changing. The loss estimated was spread as follows: ₹ 5 lakh crore in April, ₹ 4.5 lakh crore in May, ₹ 4 lakh crore in June and ₹ 2.5 lakh crore in first half of July. Local consumers had stopped going out to buy goods and those buying from nearby States had stopped doing so due to the lack of inter-city and inter-State travel. The Association was disappointed that there was no stimulus package given to the trading community. This could have been in the form of interest on loans, relaxation in payment of taxes.

CARE Ratings' study on corporate performance for Q1 reveals that net sales for a representative set of companies in this sector fell by 58.2%, the sample companies registered a loss this quarter. FICCI had conducted a survey on the impact and the results showed that the proportion of manufacturing units reporting increase in output dropped to 10% in Q1 from 15% in previous quarter. The sample included 300 manufacturing units from both large and SME companies. The sectors affected the most were auto, leather and footwear, electronics and electrical, and textile machinery.

The periodic lockdowns had an impact on the consumer goods industry. Companies such as Godrej Consumer and ITC were reportedly banking on inventories in July to meet demand. July production got affected due to local production being disrupted due to the restriction in labour movements as well as movements from their warehouses due to these lockdowns in various zones.

A JLL Survey on the Indian Hospitality Industry as on July 1 revealed the following:

- 60% of the operators surveyed believed that it will take 13 to 24 months for their portfolio to bounce back to 2019 Revenue Per Available Room (RevPAR) levels.
- 53% of the total leading hotel operators have shut down more than 80% of their inventory during the nation-wide lockdown period.
- Over 60% of respondents had up to 10% of their total hotels serving as quarantine facilities predominantly in key markets, with some of these hotels providing rooms for the "Vande Bharat Mission."
- 53% of the respondents believed that key business cities are likely to witness an early pick-up in room nights demand.

Business Today on 29th April reported that occupancy across hotels in key cities witnessed a sharp decline, as travel restrictions intensified, and India entered a nationwide lockdown towards the end of March 2020. The April edition of HVS ANAROCK Hotels & Hospitality report showed occupancy in India declining by more than half, close to 53% in March 2020 compared with the corresponding period last year. The report expected the overall revenue of the Indian hotel sector to decline approximately by ₹ 90,000 crore in 2020, reflecting an erosion of 57% compared to last year. The revenue loss in the organized segment was expected to be around ₹ 40,309 crore in 2020 and a little higher at ₹ 41,126 crore in the unorganized category, as per the revised estimates as on April 17, 2020. The revenue of the semi-organized segment was expected to decline by ₹ 8,379 crore. Moreover, the organized segment was expected to witness a 47.9% reduction in occupancy and 57.8% drop in RevPAR in 2020.

Interestingly, the *Economic Times* reported in January 2021 (January 26, 2021) that a private firm tracking the industry showed that the total room inventory occupancy for hotels in 2020 stood at 29% and the revenue per available room fell by 62% to ₹ 1423. Hotel occupancy rate was down to 39% in Mumbai, 36% in New Delhi, 32% in Chennai, 29% in Hyderabad and 25% in Bengaluru.

A PTI report on 5th July revealed that a survey of 250 start-ups showed that the Covid-19 pandemic had an unprecedented impact on the business, with 70% respondents saying that their business was impacted with some of them being forced to shut shop. 12% of the start-ups had shut operations and 60% were operating with disruptions The Survey on the 'Impact of Covid-19 on Indian Start-ups' conducted by FICCI jointly with the Indian Angel Network revealed that only 22% of the start-ups had cash reserves to meet fixed cost expenses of their companies over the next three-six months. The findings showed that 68% of the start-ups were cutting down their operational and administrative expenses and almost 30% of the companies stated that they will lay-off employees if the lockdown was extended too long.

FICCI Survey published on 21 July 2020 highlighted the following:

- Manufacturing activities had nosedived in the country to nearly one-third of the pre-Covid level.
- Manufacturers are looking to reduce dependency in areas like automotive, textiles machinery and leather/ footwear firms are looking at alternative sources of inputs/raw materials.
- On an average, companies operated between 28 to 63% of their pre-Covid capacities with workforce deployment ranging from 33 to 57%.
- The proportion of respondents reporting higher output during April-June 2020 has fallen to just 10% as compared to Q4 of 2019-20 (15%).
- A whopping 90% of respondents also said that they expect low or same production in Q1 2020-21.
- Overall, there has been a capacity utilization decline in manufacturing to 61.5% in Q4 2019-20 as compared to 76% in Q3 FY20.
- The future investment outlook looked subdued as only 22% respondents reported plans for capacity additions for the next six months as compared to 28% in previous quarter.
- Since lockdown, prices have gone up for raw material, the financing cost has risen, the issue of demand uncertainty persists along with the shortage of skilled labor and working capital. Moreover, logistics costs continue to soar. These are some of the major constraints for the expansion plans of companies.

Economic Times had reported on July 21st that the coffee chain Cafe Coffee Day (CCD) had closed down around 280 outlets in the first quarter of the current fiscal year, citing profitability issues and likely future increase in expenses, a company statement said. With these closures, the total count of its outlets stood at 1,480 as on June 30, 2020.

Lokmat (English) reported in July 2020 a Proptiger Real Insight Q2 2020 report which showed some interesting observations. A quarterly analysis of eight prime residential markets in India, only 19,038 units were sold during the period between April and June 2020, when the government had imposed strict travel restrictions to contain the virus' spread. The adverse effect of the pandemic was even more pronounced on new supply, as only 12,564 units were launched during the three-month period. In percentage terms, housing sales declined 79% annually while falling 73% QoQ. Similarly, new supply dipped 81% annually while falling 65% QoQ.

When compared to the levels seen during the same quarter last year, unsold stock declined 13% in the eight cities, primarily on account of a fall in new launches. As on June 30, 2020, developers had an inventory consisting of 7,38,335 units across these markets. In Q2 2019, the unsold stock stood at 8,46,460 units. At 55%, Mumbai and Pune markets together contributed the highest share of unsold stock, followed by NCR (15%) and Bengaluru (10%).

Inventory overhang, however, had increased to 35 months as against 28 months last year. Inventory overhang is the time developers would take to sell off the unsold stock, at the current sales velocity. The NCR market had the highest inventory overhang as of now, while Hyderabad had the lowest, at 19 months.

Rural India was not insulated from the lockdown. A study called "The Rural Report" conducted by news portal Gaon Connection and Delhi-based Centre for Study of Developing Societies showed that around 68% of the population in rural India faced a monetary crisis. Again around 78% suffered job losses because of stringent lockdown measures put in place to control the spread of the coronavirus. These findings were based on face-to-face interviews with respondents across 179 districts in India. Further 23% of the respondents were forced to borrow money to manage their expenses and 8% had to sell a valuable possession such as a mobile phone or a watch for sustenance.

Quite expectedly 28% of migrant workers were not paid for the work they had done in cities.

These vignettes are a sample of the disruptions caused across industry due to the lockdown. Clearly, there was significant pain inflicted on people as businesses went into a spin on account of the lockdown. While this can be said to be a short-term effect the psychological impact on account of these travails cannot be quantified. While some of these jobs would be restored over a period, there would be a similar proportion that would disappear forever. This holds especially in industries which are already in the presence of reinventing themselves post covid. Rudimentary practices like working from home has led to less demand for corporate space which affects the real estate sector quite perceptibly. Closures of restaurants could mean the end of several positions in this catering segment. While it will be hard to quantify the net effect, it can be surmised that alternative jobs have to be found for them. Even 5% displacement will mean four million jobs for migrants in these testing times.

Chapter 3
Migrants

There was a ragged band that followed in your footsteps
Running before times took our dreams away
Leaving the myriad small creatures trying to tie us to the ground
To a life consumed by slow decay

—Pink Floyd: High Hopes

Every nation had closed or partly closed its borders since the pandemic began. The *Economist* noted that there would have been more than 65,000 restrictions on mobility. But the costs of global immobility were very high it added. To begin with billions of cancelled journeys meant millions of jobs were lost and lives distorted which was a corollary. An example was given that as bankers and tourists stopped flying to say the Gulf area, the migrants were the first set of people to be affected. In the hospitality industry for instance, they typically 'made beds and stirred soup'. This class was laid off. Now comes the irony as foreigners without jobs were required to leave the Gulf as per the local rules. But they could not as the flights were grounded. Hence millions of migrants were stranded and as their savings depleted were left in penury. An ignominy which resulted was that some ended up begging which is criminal offence in this region and hence faced the threat of being arrested.

Further, it must be noted that even when things return to normal after say a year or so there will always be fear of foreigners who were supposedly the carriers of the virus to begin with. The people from China are being targeted in Africa and the same was meted out to Africans in China. South Africa wanted to create a fence around its border with Zimbabwe for this reason to prevent the transmission of the virus. The USA has not hidden its hostility to Chinese presence. Several countries were already under the conviction that even before the pandemic struck, migrants from other countries had taken over local jobs by underselling their services. Therefore, the Covid experience was solid ground for putting an embargo on their presence.

With the second wave of the virus spreading from September onwards in countries which looked like that they were over the pandemic these fears would remain, even though governments would not be going in for lockdowns as it has been proved that they do not really make a material difference and add to economic misery. But the migrant class for sure will be unwanted everywhere as the level of suspicion and fear will remain high.

What was the Scene for India?

The issue of migrants was probably the biggest scar in the country post the announcement of the lockdown. Over the years there was a tendency for rural-urban migration to take place as agriculture became less attractive given the vicissitudes of the weather. While the MGNREGA programme was to provide 100 days of employment to all rural folks who wanted work, it was observed that on an average people used only 50 days. While availability of works was one issue there was also the case of people wanting a better lifestyle, which led to migration to urban areas besides the metros which were in demand.

The job opportunities in the non-rural areas were enormous. First, those with least skills could go in for the construction works where the wages were attractive. With the real estate boom there were lots of job opportunities even for just carrying material. Those who had skills of plumbing, carpentry, and electrical works could get even higher wages. A minimum wage of ₹ 550-600 per day has been prescribed and the salary earned would depend on the number of days worked.

Second, the opening of the retail segment opened avenues in malls and shopping centres which gave better lives to them and with a bit of training were able to be security personnel, cleaners, employees in retail outlets, parking attendants, etc. As these facilities proliferated, their opportunities also increased manifold. Salaries could be between ₹ 12,000-20,000 per month depending on the location and the job done.

Third, those who came and gained some qualification to run machines got employed in the SMEs and jobs like bag making, lathes, auto spare parts, electrical parts, etc. became good earning avenues for them. Here the salaries could be between ₹ 10,000-30,000 per month depending on the scale of the unit and the work done.

Fourth, the success of ecommerce has been phenomenal with the delivery agents making a neat sum besides tips that are given by most customers. Food delivery personnel could earn between ₹ 40-60 per order.

This illustration of the income earned is to support the proposition that most of the migrant labourers moving to the metropolitan or urban areas are able to earn an income which is substantially more than what they could have earned in an uncertain rural farmland. As can be seen the income earned was fairly reasonable and while most of this labour huddled up in small settlements to save on housing costs, were able to remit a fairly high part of their earnings which can range from 30-60% to their homes in the rural areas. These jobs were permanent in most cases except probably menial construction jobs which were project based but tended to be continuous.

In fact, in rural India there is a lot of uncertainty as one is never sure of the monsoon, availability of irrigation and ultimately the crop prospects. Hence, when the shutdown took place, it came as a shock and with the knowledge that their business was at different stages of being shut down, the people had to look to going back to their homeland. The issue is that most of these employers were not able to pay wages or salaries when the business like say a cinema theatre closed indefinitely. At the same time, the migrants could not continue to live in rented or shared accommodation as there were no income streams to support the same. Therefore, the people perforce had to leave their place of work and move back.

There was another group of self-employed who ran stalls on the road or were vendors of household goods including fruits and vegetables. This group was acknowledged as being a fairly large class with the Atmanirbhar Bharat version 1 was announced where separate dispensation was provided to local vendors. These people had nowhere to go once there was a shutdown as their livelihood came to an end and they could not set up shop as there were restrictions on their movement. Hence, from being people who could be considered to be in the lower middle-class families, they were reduced to penury and at the mercy of a system which saw the macro but not the micro picture.

The response of the government was quite quick but not planned and lacked the human touch. The number of migrants can never be established, and the estimate could be anywhere between 10-20 million who were out of work and could not afford their accommodation in the place of work and had to move back to their villages. In fact, going by the FM's presentation made in May 2020, it was stated that the government had helped out 80 million migrants with various relief measures. This is nearly 6% of the entire population whose livelihood was in jeopardy on this score. But it was found that thousands of migrants did not get food from the PDS. This is so because some lacked the correct documentation to procure a ration card because ration cards are neighborhood-specific and are not portable. Absence of such documentation led to denial of rations.

The 80 million number is significant because this means that eight crore workers working on an average of ₹ 200 a day wage (NREGA wage) would have lost income of ₹ 1600 crore daily. For three months this works out to ₹ 1.44 lakh crore and if they were to remain unemployed for another three months would be ₹ 2.88 lakh crore or nearly 1% of nominal GDP. Intuitively, the various relief measures announced and provided for this class of people could not compensate fully and at best could have helped them tide over immediate basic necessities.

The intent of the government was positive and the following guidelines out by the Ministry of Health and Family Welfare says it all. Some of them are given below.

Migrant workers faced with the situation of spending a few days in temporary shelters, which may be quarantine centres, while trying to reach to their native places, are filled with anxieties and fears stemming from various concerns and are in need of psycho-social support. As part of such support, following measures can be adopted.

- Treat everyone migrant worker with dignity, respect, empathy, and compassion.
- Listen to their concerns patiently and understand their problems.
- Recognise specific and varied needs for each person/ family. There is no generalisation.
- Help them to acknowledge that this is an unusual situation of uncertainty and reassure them that the situation is transient and not going to last long.
- Inform them about the support being extended by Central Government, State Governments/NGOs/health care systems, etc.
- Emphasise on the importance of their staying in their present location and how mass movement could greatly and adversely affect all efforts to contain the virus.
- Reassure that even if their employer fails them, local administration and charitable institutions would extend all possible help.
- Out of desperation, many may react in a manner which may appear insulting. Try to understand their issues and be patient.
- Remind them that it is safer for their families if they themselves stay away from them.

It was clearly stated that all those who were migrants would be housed in shelters and taken care of. This meant that vast areas were covered, and beds provided in a ward like structure where people lay about doing nothing but being provided food at zero cost. The problem was that they did not know their future and just waited. Those who did not go into the shelters started moving back homewards and this is when they had to face the humiliation of being physically abused by security forces, fleeced by trucks drivers who promised to take them in overcrowded vehicles where there was no social distancing maintained or just walked for miles with their families. Some of the images shown in the media revealed the trauma that they had to go through which was reminiscent of what was the state of refugees who came to India during partition in 1947. In some places like Bareilly there were images of migrants who had returned home being asked to squat on the ground and were sprayed with disinfectant which went viral. The crowding of migrants desperate to get home in Delhi were other images which showed their plight which also showed how the establishment did little to help them.

In between there were various announcements made about allowing migrants to return home some of which were based on rumours while others were real. At any rate, these people made their way to railways stations only to be beaten by the cops for violating the curfew. When the government announced the starting of Shramik Seva trains to take them back it led to further confusion as people had to wait for their turn to get on board. As things were not well organized it led to migrants going all the way to the station and then being sent back which led to them spending time on the roads waiting for their turn. To add to their woes the guidelines set by different states meant that there were different rules for allowing migrants to move in and out. Some States stated that they would not allow migrants from Maharashtra as the State had the highest number of cases. Others had rules of quarantine for those who came in while some wanted to do the same but could not impose due to absence of testing facilities. Further, those who managed to reach their villages were ostracized as the local panchayats were wary of allowing them to come for fear of spreading the virus. This added to the trauma of families which were without money and jobs and at the mercy of the system which was trying hard but unable to provide any solace except for free fares and some nourishment for the journey which often took twice the time to reach the destination. The government had stated that 4,621 Shramik Special trains were run from May 1 to August 31, 2020, which transported 63 lakh passengers across the country.

The ferrying services became controversial as the Centre and States could not decide on the sharing of cost of these journeys and while it was stated that the migrants would not have to pay anything, delays were created by the cost-sharing controversy. This dispute between the Centre and State was to get scaled up in course of the unlock process where the Centre was not able to compensate the States for the loss in GST revenue as was promised when they signed up for the same.

There were complaints of these trains taking double the time to reach their destinations. Depending on the locations of the trains the facilities provided to the passengers were of different quality. Around the end of June this process of moving migrants carried on which ran after a point of time in parallel with the opening of limited services of the Indian Railways. Migrants had different experiences on these trains. Some complained that they ran out of food and water during the two-day journeys while others complimented the railways for treating them well. There was no uniformity for sure in terms what all had to be done for these passengers.

To get a picture of the travails of the migrants during the first two months, the following provides some highlights from a study reported on 20th June in the *New Indian Express*. The survey was carried out by the Centre for Equity Studies in collaboration with Delhi Research Group and Karwan-e-Mohabbat. The report covered casual labourers, self-employed persons, and monthly salary earners.

92% of the respondents had lost their jobs, said the survey which covered both migrant and non-migrant workers. Among those interviewed, 24.5% were women and 75.5% men.

Most of the respondents belong to Uttar Pradesh followed by Bihar, Assam, Jharkhand, and Delhi.

Over 10.5% of the over 1,400 interviewees said they were out of food for more than seven days facing an extreme hunger situation.

Around 30% of respondents said they occasionally went out of food—for one-two days, and 20% said they frequently ran out of food for four-seven days during the period of lockdown.

Among those who reported they never ran out of food said they reduced their intake and often had one meal a day. At least 5% were skipping meals to provide food for their children.

The respondents had no access to social security measures, the report pointed out. This would mean they did not lack access to institutional support amid the pandemic alone but even under normal circumstances. While around 25% had no sources of support for food during the lockdown, 43.3% received support from civil society organizations and 38.7% from the government. The government should have addressed food and livelihood concerns of workers from the day the lockdown came into effect, the study observed.

On October 9, 2020, the *Telegraph* quoted a survey carried out on "Migrant workers: A study on their livelihood after reverse migration due to lockdown" by the Inferential Survey Statistics and Research Foundation. The survey covered 2,917 returned migrants from 505 gram panchayats in 34 districts in Bengal, Bihar, Odisha, Uttar Pradesh, Chhattisgarh, and Jharkhand. It found that their average monthly income had, after their return, fallen from ₹ 13,683 to ₹ 2,045—a drop of 85%. 67.64% wanted to return to their workplaces, where—75% of them reckoned—there would be better job opportunities. The government said it had allocated an additional ₹ 40,000 crore under the MGNREGA, which promises every rural household up to 100 days' work a year. However, the survey found that while the job scheme was supposed to absorb a substantial number of the returned migrants, it provided employment to just 3.53% of them. While many of the returned migrants did casual work for an average of 4.59 days a week, nearly half were paid less than the minimum wage. About 35% had no work.

The survey found that 50% of the migrants were salaried workers before the lockdown while 42% were casual workers and the rest were self-employed. Another finding was that some States had started giving free rations to the stranded migrants during the early days of the lockdown, but it was too little. Only 4% received the free rice and less than 2.57% received free wheat and dal. The survey has found that there was hardly any support for sustaining their income or rations at their place of work.

The challenge now for the migrants who have returned is manifold. The tendency to begin with is to go back to the roots which is farming. As most of them come from farming families which may or may not be owning land, the consolation is to go back to land and help in agriculture. This has also led to higher supply of labour on limited land which exists that can be called disguised unemployment. This will be buttressed by the additional funding being provided by the government to the NREGA programme. An interesting thing about MGNREGA is the limited success during the first two months of the lockdown. The programme involves States providing jobs which are normally not formal work but what is called '*kutcha*' projects. Also, the jobs involved works like cleaning of drains which were rejected by the migrants. This is important because as mentioned earlier, most of the migrants were fairly well paid in the earlier jobs which carried a certain level of dignity in terms of skill acquisition or being proficient in dealing with customers at different levels. For them it was but natural that they rejected such projects. Also given that the wage paid was ₹ 202 for a maximum of 100 days which works to ₹ 20,200 per year compared with the ₹ 12,000-20,000 per month being earned by them.

This is one reason why there will be substantial downscaling of their living standards in the rural areas as farm income would continue to be depressed as has been observed in the last couple of years where higher output normally tends to bring down prices thus limiting the upside of a good monsoon. Add to this the limited recourse to the MGNREGA which is a stop gap facility rather than one which provides a steady stream of income. It must be remembered that MGNREGA was designed to provide employment between harvests so that farmers could have some income during this period. It was not meant to be a permanent source of income which is what is required today.

Ideally, the MGNREGA should be replaced with a more meaningful programme which weaves several other government projects especially in roads, railways, and urban development to provide work for these people.

The second issue for the migrants is whether they would be willing to go back to their place of work. The SMEs have been particularly impacted by this lockdown leading to layoffs. Services like hotels, restaurant, tourism, theatres, and transport are all the most affected segment which will take a longer time to recoup which means that demand for labour would be low. Therefore, those engaged in services activity would be able to get back to work with a lag. However, for manufacturing the picture would be different as the measures taken by the government to provide all kinds of support to the business community could help to bring about an earlier revival, though this would work over a period of time depending on the type of business involved. Construction too would be earlier to pick up as builders would like to complete the projects that were stuck due to the shutdown. On the demand side, the opportunities would be varied.

The important thing is how migrants respond to these calls from their employers. The trauma that they have been through has been quite immense and never since independence time when people migrated from Pakistan to India were such large-scale movement forced on people. The fear factor would be immense and while the end of the pandemic in India is not known it is also not clear as to what would be the steps taken by the government. This is where there has been State failure in not being able to communicate to the people as to what kind of action would be taken by the government while the pandemic lasts. Also, the recurrence of the same cannot be ruled out anywhere in the world which means that the government must decide on some action plan should this happen. The absence of communication ostensibly due to inability to plan has caused a lot of uncertainty which will lead to migrant labour remaining in their hometowns for a longer period.

There were some signals sent by some of the States that they would be helping to provide opportunities to the migrants in their territory by setting up business projects. Therefore, the idea of providing the local population with jobs in say repair shops, manufacture of parts, auto components, street vending, etc. is progressive as it would help to rehabilitate the migrants while simultaneously providing an impetus to the regional economy. This can in turn be a limiting factor for the urban/metro employers who could find it difficult to hire labour. However, as the nation went through the lockdown and unlock phases, this issue was no longer on the table and as things were allowed to return to normal this idea was never implemented meaningfully anywhere. Given that normally States tend to publicize any such actions the absence of them proves that the regional governments did not pursue such ideas once the unlock process had been announced as it was felt that the market forces would address these issues from thereon.

Hence, this critical piece of production, i.e. labour has been distorted to a very large extent by the lockdown and will change the entire dynamics of how employment evolves over time. Given that this was a man-made decision with little planning, the responsibility of the same vests with both the Central and State Governments which were unable to react with a perspective. While it is also true that one is wiser after the event, the fact that three months into the lockdown there was still no comprehensive plan to roll back the shutdown reflects the challenges in a federal structure of governance where there is no one-view on strategy.

Let us look at which sectors would be affected the most on account of loss of labour. The first one which comes to mind is construction as this is one sector which employed a large number of unskilled labourers. Construction includes roads, bridges, flyovers on the social infrastructure front which is led by government entities where contracts are given to private players. The other part is private which includes residential buildings, commercial complexes, and retail malls. The demand for such property ebbed during the lockdown period and the future remains uncertain. Demand for any of such property depends on enterprise doing well and households having an income to service their debt. Therefore, there would be a time lag here.

The problem with the builders is property under construction. Being hit by falling demand as well as high carrying cost, completing such projects is necessary. Here, getting in labour was a challenge. Governments—both Centre and States—had permitted construction work to recommence from mid-May onwards, but the problem was with labour. This was seen primarily in the public works where there was less labour to complete repair of roads or further the construction of flyovers and bridges that had gotten stalled in March. This was noticed in all urban areas where work had restarted albeit at a very gradual pace with labour availability being reduced to 10-20%. This was the time also when migrants were being ferried back to their hometowns. The sharper point here is that the more unskilled labour is required for exterior work and with the monsoon being a slow period, the possibility of labour finding jobs in the rural hinterland can affect supply of such services when things normalize.

The second segment which has gotten affected related to the retail segment which uses a large quantum of such labour to provide services in malls and other commercial complexes. As this labour is outsourced, absence of payments to the agency results in non-payment to these workers. Banks too use such labour. But as they were functioning, they have paid the outsourced agencies which in turn have compensated the workers. Therefore, all services which use semi-skilled or unskilled labour would be impacted by this workforce not returning to their place of work.

The third which is more generic is the SME sector. With labour migrating in large numbers, getting them back will be a challenge and as the state of uncertainty is very high for this sector, migrant labour will be more unsure of returning. Therefore, there will be a circular syndrome here where labour will not return unless it is sure of the work availability which in turn cannot start in a steady way in the absence of availability of labour. This problem persists even as of December 2021.

While it would be fair to say that things would return to equilibrium after a couple of years, the interim period will be one of uncertainty for this class of labour. There could clearly be a division of migrants that would return to the urban areas depending on the pace of normalcy being achieved and those that would prefer to be in their rural habitat and seek work within these confines which could be in farming or alternatively in smaller businesses in manufacturing and services. As of January 2021, there have not been any reported instances of States providing alternative permanent work for the migrants. The NREGA programme has been used for sure but is of a temporary nature as the future allocations for such a scheme are uncertain. The future of this segment will hinge on how things pan out in the urban centres where they were employed.

Chapter 4
Periodic Lockdowns

And in the end it's only round 'n round
Haven't you heard it's a battle of words
The poster bearer cried
"Listen son", said the man with the gun
There's room for you inside

—Pink Floyd: Us and Them

The fissures in a federal set up became evident from June onwards when the 'unlock 1' jargon came into use. The Central Government made it clear that there was the need to unlock the economy in a judicious manner which meant gradual. There were instructions from the top that several goods and services which were considered as being non-essential till May could be operational with conditions being imposed. While these were general guidelines, States were told to put in place the required frameworks based on their evaluation of the situation.

This was not to be as States were given freedom to unlock based on their perspectives and while the central directions on what was possible could be considered, anything forbidden at that level remained banned across the country. But what was permitted was treated differentially by States and hence some like Delhi and Karnataka opened more than say Maharashtra.

Given the federal structure, even States take a more macro view of things and it is left to the local authority which can be the municipal authority or the panchayat to take a final call.

The spread of the virus had made all regions segregated into various zones with each one carrying their own restrictions based on the incidence of the virus. Therefore, green, orange, and red zones were drawn up. Further there were modifications made to classify containment zones in each town or city which was based on the perception of the requisite authority. While the classification was more to control the spread of the virus, in effect, the business community were in limbo several times and this held especially for the SMEs which had to open and close periodically. Simplistically put while production is in one or multiple centres which have to follow local laws, the value chains on supply and demand sides criss-cross the entire nation thus crossing various States and their local laws. Given the issues in getting back labour and running business, the uncertainty was a major hindrance.

June was the time when the Central Government spoke of unlocking the economy and with a touch of the dramatic, the series got to be known as Unlock with suffixes of 1.0, 2.0 and so on. This made a lot of sense as the right way to go about this was to do so in a systematic manner where gradualism was of importance so that there was order.

The entire chain however turned out to be chaotic again which gave the impression that there were no lessons learnt from the lockdown. The lockdown exposed the fissures in the federal system where every State wanted to protect its citizens at the cost of the economy. Hence, there were restrictions on movement of goods into states on the ground that it could be infectious. This created a chasm in the instructions at the Centre and States. Business had to deal with this asymmetry and in the typical Indian way adjusted to the new setting in the first two months. The unlock programme should have plugged these gaps to ensure that things were smooth across the country.

The curious thing about the spread of the virus is that it is dependent on the number of people tested. As long as people are not tested, it is hard to guess the malaise as a large section was under what was called 'asymptomatic' group where they exhibited no signs of the virus until tested. As there was limited capacity to test given the availability of kits, the revealed numbers may not have been able to capture the true picture.

Let us see how this went in number of cumulative tests done on a monthly basis.

Date	Cumulative tests
April 9	130,790
April 30	830,200
May 25	3,033,590
June 24	7,560,780
July	14,381,300
September 2	45,509,380
October 2	76,717,000
November 11	121,962,000
December 10	151,632,000
January 14	178,401,000

Source: Statistica.com

By end May, we had tested three million people when the unlock process was invoked. Subsequently, in one month we added 4.5 million tests and as the infection levels were detected, the numbers increased thus pushing states to a spot. The problem really was that when the testing was done, there were limited kits and medical persons to conduct the same. Hence, the areas covered were limited. As the capacity was built, the testing spread to more regions and more cases came to be detected. With an infection rate of say 10% the number of cases rose exponentially. The result was that as a larger geography was covered and states which looked insulated to begin with were soon engulfed with higher infection levels. In typical Indian fashion the blame was apportioned to communities to begin with and then spread to habitats and later to migrants when they could go home. In between there were plans to bring back expats to the country which also meant that they were made responsible for the spread of the virus. The reality was that testing led to higher cases being detected with the strike rate being in the region of 5-10% as the number of tests increased.

The rise in cases in almost all places which had opened meant that the local governments panicked and imposed localized lockdowns after businesses were partially operational. The unlock covered retailers of non-essential goods, dry cleaners, beauty parlours, repair and garages and so on. Once opened, businesses tried to get back on their feet and get their labour together. Elaborate sanitization processes were brought in by establishments to ensure safety protocols were maintained. During this recovery period the State Governments came up with these lockdowns for periods ranging from 7-21 days thus upsetting the applecart. The bigger issue really is that business cannot operate with uncertainty in environment. If told to follow SOPs, they would adjust to the same. If told that the unlock would be after a month, they would reconcile to the situation. But a flip-flop is a major disturbance for any business as the road is not clear. Arrangements made to start business which includes inventory, raw material supplies, labour, transport, storage would once again tend to be distorted and push things backwards. Labour as such was going to be a tricky issue. Migrants left as their employers closed shop as they could not operate and hence pay wages. Once summoned back, they faced the same risk of being out of money if their units were closed due to local laws.

States were however fairly focussed on stopping the spread of the virus which was still believed to be controlled by lockdowns. Therefore, the impact on business was more severe for multiple times. Also, households which did display some pent-up demand, withdrew once these lockdowns took place again as the signal was that people were still to be confined to their homes.

The peculiar trait here was that the government announced unlock to preserve business which was necessary. Therefore, the environment was made more congenial for production. Hence, the supply side was addressed to an extent by opening the door even if it was only partly. What was missed is that for business to succeed finally the consumer must be there and if the customer is locked up at home, the purpose of business gets defeated. This is exactly what happened. Once again it was clear that the absence of planning afflicted the entire scene in various states. The two should have been done in conjunction. One cannot have beauty parlours operate when the users, which is the households are ensconced in their homes. It looks like that while the government had unlocked, clearly the right doors were not used.

Some of the consequences of such an unplanned unlocking process can be savoured here. *Economic Times* on 14th July reported some statements made.

> Large manufacturers and retailers of consumer goods, smartphones and automobiles said sales have declined by about a third in the past week as localised lockdowns have been rolled out across the country to arrest the spread of Covid-19. That's reversed the gains industry had made in June after the nationwide lockdown imposed in March was eased. Pune and Bengaluru are among the cities going under lockdown.
>
> Sporadic lockdowns are disrupting operations and standard operating procedures, which are different for different states.

"Weekend sales are down by 30-35%, especially in UP, Karnataka, Punjab and Indore, as markets are shut and there is no economic activity," said managing director of an India unit of German wholesale retail chain. "The one-off lockdowns are hurting the revival the industry had seen in June and first week of July. We are unable to plan inventories or promotions because different states are announcing different types of shutdowns."

Mobile phone retailers said sales in July have dropped 30-40% from June due to flattening of pent-up demand and mini lockdowns while supplies have improved. All India Mobile Retailers Association said the localised closures will hit the industry and there may not be any pent-up demand that will juice up the market when shops in these areas open.

"Whenever there is a lockdown of 7-10 days, obviously sales get impacted, customer sentiments get impacted," said the marketing head of a leading automobile company. "Bengaluru, for instance, was doing very well. But now we will lose opportunity for 8-10 days. It (lockdowns) is not in our control—we are focusing on what we can do."

Apple had to temporarily shut its national distribution centre in Bhiwandi due to the lockdown in Thane near Mumbai, squeezing supplies to offline retailers. Several other brands also have national warehouses in Bhiwandi and their networks had also been hit.

Intermittent closure and reopening of states disturbed the entire cycle of business as it takes a lot of time to streamline processes back to capacity. Reckitt Benckiser, Coca-Cola, Procter & Gamble, and Nestle among other home, personal care and healthcare makers were affected by these volatile changes. The disruptions in one state had a trigger effect on the other markets as well since there is interdependency in terms of labour and other supplies.

As late as November, states had been imposing localized lockdowns of different types. In places like Ahmedabad post Diwali, the curfew timings were between 10 in the night on Friday to 6 am on Monday for example. This may not sound significant but does disrupt business activity considerably and causes a lot of uncertainty. Businesses like restaurants, tourism, hotels, entertainment had barely opened with limited capacity permitted in October and would have to close activity during these phases. The cost imposed is high because as revenue dries up, they must bear the overhead costs which includes labour essentially. Others had banned all movement of goods and services except essentials which was a regression to the past. Therefore, there was palpable panic and a sense of lack of direction for most states which had not learnt their lessons after the first lockdown.

Curiously, Maharashtra was in dialogue at one point of time with the centre to restrict the entry of flights from Delhi as the number of infections was highest here. This seemed senseless given that passengers from Delhi would opt to come to cities in Maharashtra from other centres. The problem with such measures is twofold. First by bringing in new restrictions in the form of mandatory testing for passengers by road, rail, and air into Maharashtra from Delhi, Rajasthan, Gujarat, and Goa movement of goods gets affected once again as drivers and staff of trucks have to be tested and quarantined in case found infected. Second, it increases the level of uncertainty in business as such approaches can be repeated in other geographies too.

The ground-level reality in case of Maharashtra-based restrictions as of January was the following. Passengers flying in from any of these four States had to be mandatorily tested at the airports. Those without any symptoms could go home while those with a fever would be quarantined. Passengers coming by trains were subjected to less stringent restrictions as there was strict checking from Delhi and Jaipur but not for any location in Gujarat. There was ambiguity for those passing through Gujarat but not originating their journeys from this State. But the testing tended to be cursory in general where temperature was taken and in case was high would be put through a covid test. Otherwise, they could proceed home. And finally, those travelling by road could come through non-targeted States and escape the test. Those driving in would generally not be subjected to any test as the initial enthusiasm had led to long queues at the toll posts. Therefore, a rapid temperature check which was through the 'wave of the device' would be used to supposedly check passengers. This was problematic especially when buses crossed over where it becomes hard to carry out these checks in the absence of manpower at these stations.

There was not much thought going into these actions giving a sense that nine months after the lockdown we did not have any contingency plan in place to address issues of a second wave of virus. Even as late as the New Year's day states panicked across the country and imposed various restrictions on movement of people through what were called night curfews. Ambiguity prevailed in Mumbai for instance as to what night curfew meant. It was interpreted as one where groups of above five people could not congregate outside their homes anywhere on the streets or in restaurants post 11 pm. The solution found by the related businesses was that the celebrations started earlier and ended by 10 or 10.30 pm. The rationale for the curfew was that all festivals or celebrations have the potential to have people collect, throw caution to the winds, and spread the virus. Therefore, these rules were thought to be necessary in the metropolis. The result again was on expected lines as people started moving out of Mumbai to nearby centres and had their parties!

The absence of thorough planning can be gauged from the situation in Mumbai in February 2021. The rule of mandatory testing of passengers coming from the four states remains even while they were no longer on the list of top infected regions. Yet passengers had to get the test done. Assuming a full capacity flight of 180 passengers the cost of everyone getting the test done would be around ₹ 1.5 lakhs at ₹ 850 per test. With at least 20 flights coming from these four States the cost to society would be around ₹ 30 lakhs per day. For a month it would be ₹ nine crore. The question is: Who takes responsibility for this cost? Quite clearly, the bureaucrat in charge of such decisions has forgotten to withdraw the rule. While petitions were made to the Government of Maharashtra to dispense with this rule in February 2021 as these four States were no longer threats, the response was to add one more State, Kerala to the list. The irony was not lost as Maharashtra hosted the highest number of live cases as of February 2021! Other States should have been having restrictions on people coming from this State. But it was the other way round.

Chapter 5
The Unlock Mystery

Breathe, breathe in the air
Don't be afraid to care
Leave but don't leave me
Look around and choose your own ground

—Pink Floyd: Breathe in the Air

Unlocking of the shutdown was also done with some bit of fanfare where the Centre announced just before the start of June, July, and August the roadmap. In September and October, it was more of incremental changes with States having their discretion depending on the ground-level conditions. In November probably due to the festival season, there were no changes made with the conditions being that the October rules held. As of January, the restrictions that held were not withdrawn except through periodic curfews, which was expected after the festival season ending with the New Year celebrations were completed.

While making the stance clear was welcome as it provided direction to business as to what was possible and what was not, the major catch was the decision taken here was not binding on the States. States were told to have their own unlock process based on the prevalent conditions. This meant that the unlock at the Centre could still mean that the doors were closed in States. Hence, the Centre unlocking was a 'necessary' condition to be satisfied before States could unlock their territory. But it was not a 'sufficient' condition from the point of view of the business and hence did not mean much relief. In fact, it only added to uncertainty as most companies have a pan-Indian presence and even a SME located in Mumbai would be dealing with customers directly or indirectly across the country.

The absence of coordination was hence palpable everywhere. While the Centre said in the unlock document that decisions were taken after consulting with States, it did not mean it was binding on all. A simple thing like the night curfew which was lifted by the Centre did not find consonance among States which continued to have their ruling in place. What does this mean? Any business which is dependent on people moving out of their homes and spending money in the curfew hours would no longer be in a position to assume that there would be revenue to be made. This can hold for a rudimentary product like petrol or diesel which is used in passenger vehicles.

The important thing is that six months after the lockdown there was still a feeling that coordination was missing within the ranks of the government and there was no coherent plan in place. As far as business was concerned August unlock was not very different from the May situation where there were more prohibitions than permissions at the Central level. Quite clearly, the State had not yet grappled with the economic problem. There was just a forlorn hope that the number of infections would reduce, which did not happen as the quantum of testing increased. The approach was clearly to do fine monitoring and fine tuning, which was probably all right from the point of view of the government. But from the economic perspective it was quite clearly a major disruption with uncertainty prevailing.

What should have been done? From the point of view of business, the unlocking path should have carried more certainty. The lessons learnt from the lockdown should have been addressed before going in for an unlock. Movement of people and goods is absolutely essential to keep the economy moving. And people also include the common man who should be in a position to buy goods and services.

An issue which prevailed in Maharashtra till November was the limited access to local trains. There was dissonance between the State and the Railways on how the trains could be opened for all. Somewhere in between it was alleged that politics came into the game due to a difference in governments. The Railways were not sure how such operations could carry on without enough safety guards. Social distancing was a definite concern from the point of view of the Railways. But with permission given in other States especially for metro services, the conflict became sharp.

The need to open the suburban trains had a bearing on employment. The problem even with the unlock process on was that labour was not able to reach their places of work. This could mean a shop or a restaurant or a workshop as people staying far off could not commute easily. While the politics aspect could be an exaggeration, the fact that till Diwali time a solution was not found reflects on the fissures in communication between the Centre and States eight months after the lockdown was imposed.

The problem is really acute for services which were completed washed out due to the lockdown. A clear roadmap for various segments was called for. The prerequisite was to have an approved standard operating procedure for all services which were to be opened up. Airlines had limited movement with several safeguards which became deterrents. The problem really is that as long as airlines were not allowed to operate there was certainty that there was no revenue to be earned and certain fixed costs had to be met anyway. Once opened up, with the SOP in place, airlines tended to face higher losses as there were operating costs like that of fuel and maintenance which kicked in and with fewer passengers on board made the exercise led to higher quantum of losses for the industry. By limiting the number of flights and the occupancy rate to begin with the airline industry was in a stickier position.

Opening beauty parlours and salons was a good step as this tends to be at the lower end of the business. However, after the initial enthusiasm in flow of customers, there was stagnation in business with all the restrictions of movement in place. Quite clearly, such a business does not run exclusively on local clientele and hence those parlours which opened and had hence to bear with higher overheads were challenged with the footfalls coming down. Opening of restaurants would also have the same accompanying risks as seen in certain States where they were allowed to open. These challenges would also have to be faced once services like malls and cinema theatres open up.

The important message is that merely allowing certain economic activity to commence without certain ground rules being addressed does not make the business sustainable. As is typical in India things do even out at the end of the day which does reflect in a way the resilience of people to the systems in which we operate. The difference here is that the opening of the economy post a complete lockdown leads to a lot of uncertainty when there are periodic knee-jerk reactions by governments at different levels. This is one reason why smaller establishments especially in the services sector will take a longer time to revert to normalcy as this has been a constant struggle to do business.

As the nation moved into February 2021 and Maharashtra witnessed in relative terms a hike in the number of virus infections, the response of the State was to warn the citizens that if care were not taken, the authority would be forced to impose a lockdown. Quite clearly, neither the citizens not the government had learnt their lessons. Not surprisingly lockdowns were implemented by various States post March 2021 from April to June.

Macroeconomic Effects

Chapter 6
GDP—The First Casualty

GDP numbers insist we are doing well,
at a time when half the country is
suffering from personal recessions.

—Edward Luce

A lockdown for any reason means that people must sit at home and all economic activity comes to an end. This was the case when it was announced that the country would come to a standstill as it was hoped that the 21 days period would ensure that everyone sat at home and could hence not spread the virus. This looked logical and could not have been contested, though evidently the result was quite different. But let us look at what the lockdown meant to begin with.

Only essential goods and services were permitted which included food items. There was ambiguity on whether personal care was also included and hence while officially it was allowed by the Centre's ruling, States had their own interpretation. Hence, shops selling essential goods were allowed to remain open with restricted timings. Non-essential were ruled out. This started at the factory gate and extended to the entire supply chain till it reached the household. Automobiles, electronics, etc. were not allowed at the higher end of the scale and newspapers were forbidden as they could carry the virus. This meant that all those at the production as well as suppliers and distributors were out of work by statute. Hence, it was not just the auto manufacturer who got affected but also the entire value chain of parts which went into the vehicle that had to shut down. The dealers closed shop and all those employed had no work to do.

All services which were not essential were closed down. The railways and airlines stopped suddenly with all tickets being cancelled indefinitely. Bus transport both local and inter-State and inter-district came to a halt. Internal travel like taxis and autos stopped plying and one could take out vehicles only for doing essential work. The Oil Marketing Companies (OMCs) were left with little work to do and worked on truncated hours as demand for fuel products came down sharply.

The more 'social' services like hospitality, tourism, entertainment (including malls and cinema theatres), colleges and schools, etc. came to a grinding halt as these are the activities involve social togetherness just like public transport. Therefore, the services sector got buffeted significantly. As of December 2020, the Mumbai local train system was not open to all passengers with only a limited category of people being allowed to travel. In fact, curiously even before the shutdown was announced all services operated at lower capacity utilization as distancing norms had to be imposed and certain standard operating practices had to be adhered to. Further services like construction had to be terminated and this included both public works and private projects. Therefore, sights of incomplete road work or bridges were a common sight. Housing as well as government projects got stalled and this would mean considerable time delays in completion of projects which in turn would lead to cost escalation at a later point of time. Real estate sector which was already struggling post Real Estate Regulation Act (RERA) with several incomplete projects was pushed back further by the shutdown as business ground to a halt. As migrant labour left for their hometowns, the challenge when the 'unlock' began was getting them back to work.

India is a services-oriented economy and with all major services coming to a standstill the spectre of a near zero% growth looked imminent. While the organized sector was out of business the impact on the unorganized segment was sharper. Domestic help was out of work and had to depend on the largesse of employers. This also held for all home services like laundry and delivery people. Hawkers who come under the self-employed were out of business and those operating small units in manufacturing, repair or services were out.

The only units which were allowed to operate officially were food products related and pharmaceuticals. Here too for the month of April there was ambiguity in communication because while an edible oil producer could produce the oil, the related industries like packaging, transportation, chemicals that go in production, etc. did not have the same freedom. There were cases where the oil processor could not do business because the packing and printing material was not available. This was because of absence of planning and a top-down approach where the gaps were plugged only when the issue escalated. Until such time police high handedness prevailed with several factory owners bearing the brunt of warrants being issued or having their staff beaten for not being at home.

The absence of planning and its ill effects could be seen in case of e-commerce where the initial orders allowed these companies to function with safeguards but due to poor communication down the line and varied interpretation at state and district levels, the cost of doing business increased with hold-ups, arrests, physical treatment being meted out, etc. Online dairy products services crashed with heavy losses as the trucks could not cross borders resulting in products rotting in the cold storage trucks.

What does this chaotic situation really mean at the aggregate level? GDP growth according to the IMF World Economic Outlook which came out in April was projected at 1.8% for India which along with China was to grow at positive rates. Just at the end of March UN had again given a pat to India as being one of the drivers of the world economy in 2020. The RBI in its policy in March however drew a line of caution and quite judiciously said that it was too premature to talk of a growth number as it was not certain how the pandemic would fare and how the shutdown would pan out. The initial forecasts provided by various organizations bordered on the positive mark but remained at the modest level of 1% or so. However, as the lockdown got extended into May and further into June, it became evident that the first quarter would be a complete washout for the economy and that growth for the year would be negative for sure. The extent of the negative number would depend on how the lockdown was rolled back and whether things return to normal after September, i.e. second half of the year. The answer was uncertain as there are no firm answers. As was seen while there was an improvement in the GDP de-growth rate in Q2 relative to Q1, technically India went into a recession for the first time with two successive negative growth rates in the period April-September.

To get an idea of how GDP gets affected the logical way is to look at the various segments that comprise the total output and then take a directional view as assigning numbers is an academic exercise based on the forecaster's assumptions of when normalcy is achieved—if at all.

Agriculture is one sector that is immune largely to the pandemic as the rural areas tend to be less prone to the spread of the virus and prediction can proceed based on the normal conditions of how the monsoon fares. Therefore, the farm sector was to be the driver for this year for sure and assuming the weather conditions are positive, higher growth rate could be maintained. The fact that migrant labour had returned to the native land means that labour supply would in abundance and sowing can proceed at a faster pace. Also, to the extent that it is possible to spread the acreage due to more labour being available, it could be a blessing.

However, the challenges here were that the mandis had to be operative. Farmers had to find way to reach the mandi with their produce which became a challenge in some States where there were restrictions on movement. Also the buyers had to be in the market and when processors, who are the bulk purchasers, were non-operational for most of the time, often farmers had to return without a sale. Hence, there was a modicum of volatility in their incomes during the rabi harvest time.

Mining with a weight of 2.3% in GDP is a sector dependent on availability of labour as well as demand for the final product. With demand slowing down considerably through the year, and labour being wary of uncertainty the sector was to get into the negative territory in terms of growth. Restrictions being imposed on movement of people put hurdles when it came to opening the mines which remained close for the first two months of the year. The global recession meant also that all minerals related to products that are exported would witness a major setback.

Manufacturing with a weight of around 16% in GDP was one of the biggest casualties. The industries that have positive scope are food related, pharmaceuticals specifically while other infra-related like metals, cement, and machinery would be contingent on other sectors reviving which could take 6-12 months. Cement for example would be dependent on how construction fares which in turn depends on government spending and prospects of the real estate sector. All of them had been pushed back due to the shutdown on both the demand and supply sides.

Electricity generation was another victim of a slump in GDP growth as commercial consumption is directly linked with the pick-up in economic activity. The shutdown had increased domestic consumption as the households were home-bound and used more power. Also working from home meant that demand for power increased. However, this was not an unmixed blessing for the power companies as the commercial rates subsidize the household rates and a shift in demand actually increases the losses of the DISCOMs. Hence, a shutdown puts the power sector under pressure. It was not surprising that growth was negative in the first quarter and it was only in September that a positive growth rate was attained. In April, May, and June output had fallen by 22.9%, 14.8%, and 10% respectively.

Construction was a washout as the conundrum surfaced along the way. The first month meant a total shutdown where all projects came to a halt. As such April is a lean season when it comes to government projects, but the deep shock was palpable where all those in process got stalled. This was accompanied by rural migration as labour moved back home or wanted to due to absence of work and hence income. Announcing the commencement of projects was staged and varied across states which again meant that when demand for labour went up the same set of people who worked were just about able to reach home. Therefore, the spectre of incomplete projects increased in this set up.

The category of trade, transport, hotels, and restaurants has a weight of around 6% in GDP and is probably the one that was most sharply impacted by the lockdown. While trade was permitted in essential goods, the plethora of rules and amendments and variations across States made a mess of this sector. Wholesale markets had challenges in terms of the number of buyers and sellers coming down to 10-20% of normal. Retail outlets could not operate in most parts of the country due to the State laws which allowed only essential goods to be sold.

As activity slowed down the transport sector too got affected and became self-reinforcing. As transport drivers and support staff fled to their villages, there were fewer vehicles to transport goods which affected trade of both agricultural and manufactured goods. Getting the drivers back was the major challenge as the unlock process started gradually and operators were not able to run their vehicles due to the non-availability of drivers.

Hotels were out of business for three months to begin with and several properties in cities were converted to isolation centres. The concern at that time was that this move would have ramifications post normalcy as there would be a stigma attached to such hotels by potential guests. Restaurants were able to offer only delivery services and the dine in facility took a longer time to reopen which was post October in some States with several limitations. Resorts and other hotels would find their business affected on account of fear among both business and leisure travelers. Hence, there is a major destruction of value here and it would take over a year for any recovery.

Transportation is a mixed bag. Airlines were operative in a limited manner and their pace of recovery would depend a lot on how patrons behave. The restrictive beginning was clearly meant to filter out those who want to travel for leisure. It is meant more for those who have to get back to their homes where it is necessary. The quarantine rules that were imposed to begin with by the government ensured that only those who have to travel would do so. Business travelers which is the bulk of air traffic would take a longer time to recover. In Q1 of the year almost all companies were working with losses and the last thing they would like to do for a year is to allow travel when the same meetings can be conducted over the web which has caught on. In fact, the new normal of working from home has also brought in the culture of having business meetings through webinars, which though may not be as effective is acceptable.

Railways also had to decide when to open up without any restrictions. Until such time it was being used more by those who have been displaced from their home territory and would have to get back to safety. The practice of going on holidays or even occasions relating to family has been pushed back significantly and hence will again take time to regain confidence. The puzzle for the government is how best to open up when the number of cases is increasing manifold. Railways is one mode which cannot maintain social distancing which is the key to controlling the virus. While by November most rail services were restored with few restrictions, the metropolitan local services were still closed to the general public with only those belonging to the essential services allowed to travel.

The banking sector has been theoretically insulated from the lockdown and has been functioning normally for most time. However, business has been affected quite sharply of risk aversion and hence growth in credit has been subdued as banks have to grapple with other issues as moratorium and handling of government priorities like SME lending. Therefore, while positive growth is expected, this cannot drive the economy for sure.

Real estate witnessed a major showdown in the first two quarters. First, projects have gotten stalled. Second, labour has disappeared and getting them back will be a major challenge given the fear psychosis. Third, demand has fallen especially in the metro cities and other urban areas as people have less purchasing power. Fourth, several individuals have gone in for moratorium which while bringing in temporary stability could be a major problem later in case the buyers are unable to maintain their jobs or receive normal income. On the commercial side with malls and other shopping areas coming under restrictions demand has slumped and given the uncertainty of normalcy will take time to get restored. Companies will not be too eager to buy property and with working from home becoming a norm to some extent, even such flexibility being given to 10% staff will reduce demand for property significantly.

There was some improvement noted around Diwali time in the real estate sector where the number of sales increased. This would compensate partly for the loss in the first half. However, the impact of such demand destruction would be seen in the coming quarters where there would be a slide after the initial pent up demand phase ebbs.

Therefore, demand destruction was all encompassing due to the announcement of the shutdown. While recovery will be at different times for different business activities, the change in mindset as mentioned earlier in the way in which business is conducted will be more important and can change the entire landscape of business. This cannot be conjectured as of now but will evolve over a period of time as all companies review their options on things like labour force, technology, travel, business deals and conferences, property, etc.

How did GDP Growth Fare in Q1 FY21?

The table below gives the growth rates of various segments of GDP for the first quarter of the year.

Growth in value added (%) 2011-12 = 100

	Q1 FY20	Q1 FY21
Agriculture and forestry	3.0	3.4
Mining	4.7	– 23.3
Manufacturing	3.0	– 39.3
Electricity, gas, water	8.8	– 7.1
Construction	5.2	– 50.3
Trade, transport, hotels, restaurants	3.5	– 47.0
Finance, real estate	6.0	– 5.3
Public, administrative services	7.7	– 10.3
GDP	5.2	– 23.9

Source: CSO

As can be seen in the table, growth rate was negative in all segments barring agriculture. Even in case of the public administration, defence, and other services segment growth rate was negative as government expenditure was more in the nature of transfer payments while other services like education, entertainment, travel, etc. were out of bounds.

A more startling factor here can be seen on the expenditure side, where there was a fall in consumption and investment as the table below shows. GDP growth by expenditure was negative for consumption and investment. Consumption was due to the inability of households to buy goods and services for two months. Investment fell as companies were not operational and as mentioned earlier project work came to a halt. While it could be logically expected that these numbers would recover as the economy was unlocked, growth would be deferred by a few quarters which is crucial for us as FY20 was a low growth year.

GDP by Expenditure (%)

Growth rates	Q1 FY20	Q1 FY21
Consumption	8.5	– 24.5
Investment	7.9	– 47.9
Government	9.5	20.2
Ratios		
Consumption to GDP	58.5	57.1
Gross fixed capital formation to GDP	28.9	19.5

Source: CSO

Now, the case of GDP growth falling was common to almost all countries including India. The issue attained a political angle when a comparison was made with growth rates in other countries. There is however a different method which is used when calculating GDP growth rates in other countries where the comparison is over the previous quarter rather than the previous year as is done in India with the seasonal factors also being addressed. This was finally clarified by the IMF which put in comparable figures to show the true picture.

April-June growth (%)

China	12.3
S. Korea	3.2
Indonesia	6.9
Australia	7.0
Japan	7.8
Russia	8.9
USA	9.1
Holland and Brazil	9.7
Turkey	11.0
Canada	11.5
EU27	11.7
Italy	12.8
France	13.8
Mexico	17.1
Spain	18.5
UK	20.4
India	25.6

Source: Gita Gopinath on Twitter

Quite clearly, the growth performance has been the sharpest in the downward direction.

The second quarter GDP numbers did show an improvement and reflects the economy being unlocked gradually. But as can be seen, overall degrowth continued albeit at a slower pace in this quarter. Here too it can be pointed out that an upward bias has been lent by the methodology followed by the CSO which uses value added numbers from the profit and loss accounts of companies. In Q2, there was a tendency for sales to fall as demand was lackluster, but companies had saved on costs by cutting back labour expenses. This was probably not the right way to increase value addition which is defined as sum of gross profit and salaries which are the returns to various factors of production.

Growth in GVA in Q2

Growth %	Q2-FY20	Q2-FY21
Agriculture and forestry	3.5	3.4
Mining	– 1.1	9.1
Manufacturing	0.6	+0.6
Electricity, gas, water	3.9	4.4
Construction	2.6	– 8.6
Trade, transport, hotels, restaurants	4.1	– 15.6
Finance, real estate	6.0	– 8.1
Public, administrative services	10.9	– 12.2
GDP	4.4	– 7.5

Source: CSO

On the expenditure side, the table below provides an overview of the growth in the three main components of GDP.

GDP by Expenditure at Current Prices (%)

	Q2 FY20	Q2 FY21
Consumption	8.9	– 7.7
Investment	– 1.6	7.0
Government	17.5	– 18.0
Ratios		
Consumption to GDP	60.2	57.9
Gross fixed capital formation to GDP	26.5	25.7

Source: CSO

In the second quarter, there was degrowth in consumption, investment, and government consumption even as overall degrowth in GDP was of a lower magnitude compared with Q1. The reason for consumption to still degrow was the existence of the lockdowns and restrictions on movements of people which affected this variable. While most non-services were opened up, the crux was getting people to spend money which was still difficult. This created an anomaly between production and consumption. Production was better placed more in anticipation of household spending which was to materialize in the festival season. While the festivals had started from August onwards, the restrictions had come in the way of spending. Hence, there was preparation for the second half of the year when festivals like Dussehra, Diwali, Christmas, and the New Year would spur additional spending. Investment too was down as data from the government accounts suggests that spending was controlled given the fiscal slippage. Private investment was still down as industrial production was low leading to low utilization levels. Infrastructure investment too was downbeat from their side given the uncertain future. The government had become cognizant of the declining revenues which also gave rise to the rather acrimonious debate between the Centre and States on GST compensation. This has led to certain cutbacks in expenditure which finally got reflected in these numbers.

The quarterly numbers for various aspects of GDP would tend to be better for sure. The loss of output and investment however in the first half would be that much more difficult to compensate. The pent-up demand for several goods and services have materialized in the third and fourth quarters but would not be able to make up for the initial loss. Besides while output can be back to the normal path in course of time, the disruption to employment and the way in which business is conducted will change as is discussed elsewhere in the book that leads to a different kind of creative destruction.

The CSO had projected a fall of 7.5% in GDP for the year in its first advance estimates published in January 2021. The final number will be more of academic interest as it could finally be within a range of plus or minus 2% as these statistics are prone to substantial revisions in the next two years as more data becomes available. But one thing is sure in terms of interpretation which is that there has been a fall in GDP which goes lower than the FY20 number which was anemic being also influenced by the last week lockdown syndrome. The implication is that a full year has been lost in terms of value addition in the economy and this also means that whatever growth is witnessed in FY22 would at best bring us back to where we were on the eve of the lockdown. Hence with GDP being around ₹ 146 lakh crore in

FY20, it would mean a decline to around ₹ 135 lakh crore and the cost of lockdown would be around ₹ 10-11 lakh crore. This is in terms of value addition which has been lost that translates to a decline in gross output by around ₹ 14-15 lakh crore. Loss in output means loss of income and hence purchasing power of the economy and goes along with job losses and reduction in income across the working class. At the secondary level, fall in consumption affects capacity utilization and hence defers investment decisions as uncertainty persists on the future course of the economy. This can be the rough cost of lockdown in terms of loss of output and income in FY21.

Chapter 7
Job Destruction

I tried so hard and got so far
But in the end it doesn't even matter
I had to fall to lose it all
But in the end it doesn't even matter

—Linkin Park: In the End

The lockdown announced meant that all activity had come to a standstill with few exceptions. Even the exceptions were not explained clearly and by the time clarity came in another two months were spent blowing hot and cold over what was possible and not feasible. This led to a major dilemma for all business units. What had to be done with labour?

Firms and workers in every part of the world have been affected by the COVID-19 shock. The ILO estimated that global labour income has declined nearly 11% or US$3.5 trillion in the first three quarters of 2020. As a result of income losses, World Bank estimated that as many as 150 million people could be pushed into extreme poverty by 2021. Without timely assistance and swift policy action, otherwise healthy firms will be shuttered permanently, and people will suffer longer.

Stoppage of activity meant that there was no production of a good or service. More importantly there was no indication given of what was the future as the lockdown went with suffixes of 1, 2, 3, etc. Therefore, companies lived with uncertainty. There were strong statements made by the PM that jobs should not be lost.

However, at the commercial level, how could one pay salaries when there was no income? Therefore, there was a movement towards two approaches taken by companies. The first was to go in for layoffs as it was not possible to pay salaries. This held for the SMEs and the services which lived literally on daily sales. Even restaurants were allowed deliveries only which meant that the large retinue of staff which served was redundant. The second, which became popular in most corporates was to announce cuts in salaries. This could be for one month or three months cut in pay or a percentage of salary. Some of the larger companies said that they would be no cuts as they could afford the same. But post two months they had to reword their thoughts when losses mounted. In fact, there were defaults on rent and other expenses where there was outsourcing involved. This affected the third-party staff. This was the story for the organized labour.

In case of unorganized labour which worked on daily wages, the scene was disastrous as they could not step out to work and their work venues were closed for indefinite periods. This led to the challenge of migrant labour across the country which was probably the biggest mess that took place. This set of people were lodged in relief camps to begin with where different government bodies and NGOs provided food and shelter to them. But once the cost became unsustainable and the people restless from being away from home for two months, they could travel back. But they had to return.

Let us look at the job scene based on reports published by various media. These are based on news reports that were highlighted at that point of time. A rider must be made that these may or may not have finally materialized or could have been reversed subsequently. These reports hence are revelations made in a particular context.

Business Insider on 13th June reported the following. Shoppers Stop was the latest to lay off over 1100 employees. Raymond had gone in for such an exercise with respect to employees and a survey of myhiring.com said 49% was the ratio of layoffs in the retail and FMCG sectors.

Scroll on May 20th had reported that Ola said the company would lay off 1,400 employees. Twitter-backed ShareChat, an

Indian video-sharing social networking service, laid off 101 employees as it expects the advertising market to be unpredictable this year as *Economic Times* reported. United States-based commercial real estate company WeWork said that it laid off 100 employees, or 20% of its workforce in India, in an attempt to cut costs and revamp operations which Reuters reported. Food delivery company Swiggy announced that it would lay off 1,100 employees, or nearly 14% of its total workforce, after demand for online food ordering dipped significantly in the past two months. Further, Indian restaurant aggregator Zomato on May 15th laid off 13% of its workforce and said it would implement salary cuts of up to 50% across the organization for at least six months.

A report said that cab aggregator Uber had decided to sack 500 to 700 employees from its India office due to a sharp decline in revenues. The firm has also decided to sack around 6,500 employees globally.

The big one was Reliance Industries which announced pay cuts of up to 50% for some top oil-and-gas division employees on April 30. Employees earning more than ₹ 15 lakh a year will face a 10% cut while senior executives will have to take 30% to 50% salary cuts.

Oyo Rooms said it would cut the salaries of all employees by 25% for four months and sent some of its people on leave with limited benefits, Reuters reported. Earlier in April, the company had laid off thousands of employees in the United Kingdom and the United States.

ThePrint on 12th June reported that thousands of retired Indian Railways' employees who were re-engaged last year are set to lose their jobs as the transporter looks to cut its expenses to ease the lockdown hit. The jobs in question involve the junior-most staffers, involved in operations such as track machines, bridge and similar technical safety categories. The pension they are entitled to is 50 per cent of the salary they get.

The newsminute.com on 26th April reported the following relating to the media which is quite significant. *The Hindu* announced pay cuts for those earning above ₹ 6 lakh per year. Those earning between ₹ 6 lakh and ₹ 10 lakh per annum would see a pay cut of 8%; those earning between ₹ 10 lakh and ₹ 15 lakh would see a cut of 12%; ₹ 15 lakh to ₹ 25 lakh is 16%; ₹ 25 lakh to ₹ 35 lakh is 20%; and those earning above ₹ 35 lakh would see a cut of 25%.

In a letter sent to employees, Hindu Group CEO said that whole time directors on the Board and independent directors have voluntarily taken cuts as well.

NDTV announced that apart from those earning less than ₹ 50,000 per month, salaries will be cut across the board, with progressively higher cuts depending on salary. In an email to employees, NDTV said that those earning the most will take the biggest cuts, and each employee was separately sent an email about their pay cut.

Earlier *Hindustan Times* cut the take home pay of employees. According to Newslaundry, an email sent to the staff by HT Media CEO said that the national newspaper was losing ₹ 3.5 crore a day as it was incurring costs without the revenues. Instead of cutting pay, the company made a part of employee pay variable. It is important to note, however, that employees rarely get their full variable pay. Variable pay can be linked to the employee's performance, as well as the financial performance of the company.

From April 1, HT said that 5% of the salary earned by those whose CTC (cost to company) is ₹ 6-10 lakh would be variable. For those earning between ₹ 10 lakh and ₹ 20 lakh, 10% will be variable, and for people earning above ₹ 20 lakh, 15% will be variable. This will not affect those earning below ₹ 6 lakh.

The *Times of India* group also instituted pay cuts for its main newspaper. For *TOI*, the group said that the variable pay/incentive to be given at the end of Q1 of FY 21, which ends in June, would be deferred, and will be reviewed later. Increments have also been deferred and will be reviewed at the end of Q2 depending on business.

On 1st July, *Economic Times* reported that IndiGo India's biggest carrier by market share, will lay off 10% of its workforce, its chief executive said in a note, as airline operators globally take a beating due to the Covid-19 pandemic and resultant shutdowns.

IndiGo currently had about 28,000 employees, of which 40% are pilots and cabin crew. A senior executive said pilots at the airline won't be affected by this move yet.

Indiaretail.com on 30th June reported that The Retailers Association of India (RAI) has estimated about six million jobs losses in the retail sector in the coming months due to the Coronavirus impact. "About 40% of the six million employees working in India's modern, rather than traditional, retail sector could likely lose their jobs in the next four months if the government does not intervene. As per recent RAI survey findings, retailers expect layoff about 20% of their manpower. Small retailers are expecting to lay-off 30% of their manpower; going forward, this number falls to 12% for medium retailers and 5% for large retailers," was the view.

Several newspapers closed editions in various centres due to the inability to be able to print and sell physical copies. This was further exacerbated by the fall in advertising revenue as the companies which used to use the media for publicity were not operating even at reasonable levels. This made staff redundant and the resulting excess supply of journalists could not be absorbed by the running establishments which were barely able to survive and had to invoke a cut in the headcount. This may be a permanent reduction as it looks very unlikely that these publishing houses would restart business editions which were closed due to non-viability at least for the next five years or so. This also included Indian language editions of business newspapers which were opened when the focus was on expansion into new cities as well as language editions.

The Ministry of Civil Aviation noted that for the period March 2020 to July 2020 there was a decline in number of employees from 1.89 lakhs to 1.72 lakhs spread across airlines, airports, ground handling and cargo operators. Ground handling saw the biggest decline from 37720 to 29254. A further update provided in the Rajya Sabha revealed that between March and September, there were 39,000 jobs lost in this segment. Airlines was down from 74,887 to 67,906, airports from 67,760 to 48,513, ground handling from 37,720 to 25074. In case of cargo operations, it was lowest from 9,555 to 9,385.

These are examples of some of the pay adjustments made by companies in the light of the lockdown. This does not include an automatic loss of salary for employees where there are variable pay packages as part of CTC which is given at the end of the year on the basis of performance of the company and employee. As all companies are likely to go down under in FY21 with losses being the rule, it will automatically mean that they will lower the variable pay of employees. Given that these can range from 5-30% depending on the cadre and the nature of the job, there would be a significant reduction in the pay received by most employees even without official pay cuts being announced. Those in the public sector where there are no variable scales could be better off unless decisions are not taken to lower the pay. At times there is mandatory donation of one day leave to the PM CARES Fund which in a way is kind of pay cut. Hence, there are different modalities in which purchasing power of workers get affected.

(*All the examples given in this chapter are from reports which were from various web sites and are not checked for authenticity. The idea is to give an idea of the various measures invoked on the employee side by various companies. These measures may not have been fully invoked or could have been withdrawn or diluted subsequently.*)

The ADB-ILO study on youth employment crisis brought out in August revealed the following:

- In India, two-thirds of firm-level apprenticeships and three quarters of internships were completely interrupted.
- The equivalent of 4.1 million youth jobs may be lost.
- In the six-month scenario, job losses for youth may equal 6.1 million in India.
- Distribution of job losses of youth to be concentrated in seven sectors: agriculture, construction, retail inland transport, textiles, hotels.

CMIE reported in September that for the period May-August there was a decline of six million white-collared workers relative to the same period in 2019. Hence, the impact even on the higher echelons was significant. Further an estimated 21 million salaried employees have lost their jobs by the end of August. There were 86 million salaried jobs in India during 2019-20. In August 2020, their count was down to 65 million. The deficit of 21 million jobs is the biggest among all types of employment.

A survey carried out by Azim Premji University for the period October-December showed that almost one out of five workers in the informal sector were either out of the labour market or were unemployed. While 3% were unemployed and 4% were out of the labour market in February 2020 which was pre-covid times, during the lockdown 61% were unemployed and 10% out of the labour market. And compared with the post lockdown period 11% are still out of the market and 8% are unemployed. These numbers are based on a very conservative definition of employment where even one day in the previous month constitutes being not unemployed.

One way of looking at the impact on employment due to COVID is to see how the salary bill of corporate India moved during the first quarter of the year. This will consider several factors which go into its constitution. The salary bill is a useful indicator as it is a combination of various inputs: headcount, increase in salary in the form of increment, payouts for the previous year in the form of bonus or variable pay. Therefore, any increase in this bill will broadly tell us about how corporates have dealt with their staff costs due to the lockdown. Layoffs is the most obvious decision taken on which few companies reveal the numbers. Very often this is euphemistically done in the form of rationalization of the workforce due to performance or rather underperformance.

Pay cuts are normally internal issues and rarely will companies openly state in the Annual Reports that they have lowered their salaries by a certain level. Hence, this is something which will be a part of the lower salary bill. Similarly, in these difficult times companies have also cut down on increments for the year which normally range between 6-10% on an average in normal years. Another way of controlling staff cost is the rationalization of the variable pay that is given in the private sector. This has become a norm of late with 5-40% being the variable component of a person's remuneration package. These numbers have been rationalized on grounds of the company not doing well rather than covid and hence would technically be under the normal process of operations and not a specific exercise.

To get a flavour of how the staff cost bill has moved, the table below provides information on the staff cost for the first two quarters of the year for a random set of 2957 companies. The IT and banking and finance sectors have been excluded as these were two industries which worked at a satisfactory level during the lockdown with the former not requiring too much of office activity while the latter was considered to be essential services and hence excluded from the curfews. This sample is only illustrative of what the situation looked like for these companies and excludes the SME segment which is largely unorganized and does not enter such samples.

₹ crore

	Q1	Q2
Salary bill 2019-20	79,523	80,525
Salary bill 2020-21	73,759	76,772
% change	– 7.2	–4.6
Absolute change	– 5,764	–3,751

Source: Author's Calculation

There has been a decline in the salary bill of the corporate sector as represented by this set of companies. In incremental terms, the total fall for the two quarters was around ₹ 9500 crore which would go up in case the entire universe is considered.

The point really is that while there have been two sets of strong arguments on employment where one school has spoken of sharp revival in job creation, while the other has highlighted increased unemployment (CMIE), the fact that the salary bill has fallen show the impact on potential consumption. Quite clearly, this has been brought about by a combination of headcount management as well as compensation. In fact, corporate performance for the first quarter was abysmal on both sales and profits. For the second quarter, sales growth was negative while profits was positive and this was mainly due to severe cost cutting reckoned by companies which involved lowering of salaries.

While it is possible that there would be restoration of salaries as industries get back to normal, it would be reasonable to assume that this would take a lot of time and get spread over the next couple of years. The employment path would be uneven and tilted against the non-financial-non-IT services sector in particular.

Interestingly, the government in October had announced that it would be releasing the bonus of ₹ 3737 crore to over 30 lakh employees for 2019-20. This means that the government did not or could not pay the same on time to its employees to the mismatch of revenue flows with expenditure. The amount to be released was presented as a means to enhance purchasing power before Diwali which was hence not a new announcement but a payment that had been deferred for over six months. Hence, even the government employees were not spared the wrath of the lockdown and while the regular salary came in one component, i.e. bonus was paid later.

What does job losses and pay cuts mean? The combination is quite lethal to the Indian growth story which was afflicted by a demand side problem even before the pandemic set. By lowering the purchasing power through these measures, the overall absorption capacity of the economy would get affected thus pushing back growth by another year for certain. It is not surprising that there is a lot of hope being pinned on the farm sector to be the driver of growth on the assumption that a good monsoon and kharif crop will lead to higher income and spending power of the farmers.

Further these cost savings measures invoked by the companies also means that the theory of pent-up demand which was being backed to bring about surge in production post the pandemic may not be realized as people will not have money to spend. It was not surprising that there has been considerable volatility in the production numbers. The irony is that when a large set of companies decides to go in for downsizing or reduction in salary it affects the spending power of the same set of households which tend to be part of the 'consumer demand' scenario. At a time when retail borrowers are taking recourse of moratorium provided by banks on loan servicing it is hard to have the same set of people go in for fresh buying of homes or automobiles through bank loans. Therefore, the growth prospects for industries like automobiles, durable goods, electronics, garments, etc. which come under the category of discretionary spending gets pushed back to a large extent on this score.

The other problem of job losses is more futuristic where those displaced may not be willing to get back to work. This holds especially for the migrant labour that has been demoralized on account of the hardships that they had to go through for poor planning.

Looking ahead, the way companies function from now on will be different. Those that have lost labour may be looking for other ways of carrying on business through higher investment in technology. The pandemic was unexpected, and companies may like to prepare for such occurrences in future by buffering from the same. This will mean that the issue of labour force will be reconsidered and lines drawn where there can be less dependency in this area.

The prolonged lockdown was followed with an unlock in June. This meant that it was possible for some businesses to start operations. However, this went along with the localized lockdowns which again pushed back business to a large extent. This meant that companies which thought were able to move towards normalcy with the unlock were further clouded with uncertainty which led to staff being in a state of flux. Labour demand is linked to production and if the latter is uncertain it become difficult to maintain the human resources leading to cuts in income as well as layoffs. Therefore, in the manufacturing sector in the SME segment, employment decisions are still challenging.

Services have been only partly opened up and sectors like media, entertainment, hotels, tourism, etc. are still not fully opened up. In the hospitality industry, the forced lockdown has led to closure of restaurants in metro centres as they were not able to bear the rent cost while labour was sent home. With permanent closure, this class of employees would have to look at alternatives.

Therefore, restoring employment count is going to be a challenge in the coming years and will be linked with the pace of recovery in the economy and the rate of economic growth in different sectors. Job creation will trail in the services sector.

Chapter 8
SME Saga of Never-Ending Woes

No society can surely be flourishing and happy, of which the far greater part of the members are poor and miserable.

—Adam Smith

The SMEs are a very important part of our economic narrative because of the contribution to the economy. The official statistics read as follows. There are 63 million such units in both manufacturing and services and account for 30% of India's nominal GDP and 45% of manufacturing output. They employ roughly around 131 million people (MSME Census in 2016) and contributed to 48% of India's exports in 2018-19. However, they are completely unorganized except where there are special zones which have been set up. They have severe problems of funding, receiving payments, limited governance standards given that they are driven by an individual/families, very small in scale and often not scalable, linked completely with larger units, limited skill sets available and above all are large job creators as wages paid are low.

This sector is always at the centre of all economic policies just like agriculture. There are hence a lot of measures on providing credit including the Mudra loans which ensure that there is a certain quantum of credit going there. Also, this sector comes under the priority sector lending tenet of banking and hence the institutional set up is very much in place and has been so for a long time now. More recently post demonetization and GST which put them in a tight spot, the RBI and the government have helped to restructure their debt so as to enable them to service them over a period of time. In February 2020, it was decided to allow for one-time restructuring of SME loans subject to certain conditions where the scheme had to be implemented by December 2020. In August on account of the special conditions that were prevalent, the scheme was extended to March 2021.

Also, the government has in place several measures to make them stronger such as laying down rules for public procurement, starting the Government e Marketplace (GeM) website, ensuring that their receivables are lowered, etc. Therefore, attention on their sustainability and growth has been at the forefront of all government policies.

Let us try and typify a MSME. It can be a sole proprietorship and can employ between 1-20 workers on an average basis. The unit would be in the unorganized sector and can be tracked if it is GST registered. There are no hierarchy structures, and the owner calls the shots. Hence, the employees would tend to be non-professionals with a couple of better educated persons from outside the family in case the size is bigger. Otherwise, it would be straight from the owner and the concept of professionalism is missing. The working hours would be typically long and most of the labour would be of the working class running the machines or providing the service (repair or servicing of TVs, bore pumps, etc.). The labour is normally paid a competitive rate and hence could be earning anywhere between ₹ 200-800 per day and hence depending on the number of days worked would earn a fairly good salary. They would however not necessarily get the benefit of the labour laws in terms of number of hours or holidays and could vary depending on the type of enterprise.

But the entire job process is well linked from procurement to sale including marketing. Often for manufactured products the link is with the bigger manufacturer. The common example is the automobile company which sources parts from SMEs where certain standards are maintained. Therefore, often there is a buyback arrangement with the seller of the final product. If the product is a final one like a fan or a watch or tubelight the links with the final retail outlet are also well established.

Therefore, the value chains on both sides are well defined. While the labour is paid a market rate to ensure that they are better off than they were in the homeland and do not switch jobs, they are for all practical purposes on their own and hence get together and live together with others like them in single rooms. Often in Mumbai for instance, they stay in shifts as they work in shifts. Therefore, their lives are well structured, and their savings are often transmitted to their families back home.

Now what did the shutdown mean for them? Overnight there was an announcement that nobody could move out from their homes and all offices were closed. This included all workshops and factories, and the only exception was essential goods. As has been discussed earlier even here there was no clarity as often the police forces came down heavily with force on those who ventured for work even in this exempted category of goods and services. But maybe 90-95% of these SMEs came to a halt by the end of March. With no production of a good or service being permitted by the government in April the backlash was felt across the value chain with the baton finally coming back to the SMEs.

First, the individual units were out of production and given that they work with little scope for holding inventory and earning revenue on a virtually daily basis if not linked with value chains, a lockdown meant zero revenue.

Second, as wages are paid based on production and revenue, a stop in the former meant that they were out of work with no income to keep them going.

Third, with no clear indication of when the shutdown would end after the extension took place, the owners had no option but to let go labour as their future was uncertain.

Fourth, where the units were linked to the supply chain, conditions were no better. If an auto manufacturer stopped producing a car or a scooter, the demand for parts came down as the limited production was supported by inventory. Therefore, the MSME unit was redundant in this situation as the upward link was broken as the final producer faced similar problems and had to also let go labour in this connection.

Fifth, related to the value chain, if the final seller was not able to make a sale, then it was handicapped by revenue not being earned which made it difficult to pay their vendors and hence the MSME faced the problem of rising receivables.

Sixth, the MSME meanwhile had been borrowing from both formal and informal sources to finance working capital requirements. Now non-receipt of payment and rising receivables meant that their indebtedness increased and there was greater demand for funding. This was where the RBI helped in March by extending the working capital limits which worked well for them as they were hard pressed for funding.

Being unorganized and fully dependent on other links in the economy the entire segment of SMEs was at a disadvantage. The links went along with migrant labour and other associated problems. As there are a large number of self or family employed businesses especially in the services sector, the shutdown has meant three months of inactivity and zero income. While the Central Government opened up non-essential services in June, States had their rules which meant that different guidelines were laid down across the country. Conditions such as working on alternative days with limited working hours became the norm for non-essential goods and services. Further with the fear factor pervading the country with the messaging being that entry of service people from outside was dangerous, households kept away from the set of SME service providers such as repair, laundry, installation, etc. Add to this the population of street side vendors that were treated with a heavy hand for the first two months, another set of MSMEs in the service sector were out of money.

What has been the relief provided to these people? The government's economic package had the SMEs at the forefront and made some announcements on the flow of credit. However, there was nothing on the demand side as such which gave them money besides what was provided to all migrants in the form of shelter with the fixed quantity of food grains and cash for a fixed period of time. The thrust was more on improving the flow of credit to the MSMEs and in order to do so the banks were to be the facilitator.

Lending to SMEs is not really anything novel as such loans are part of the priority sector where targets are set for banks. However, the evolving situation is such that banks are not predisposed to lend beyond what they should to this sector. The reason is simple. The SMEs have been buffeted twice already by the policy of demonetization followed with the reform of GST. This stressed out their business and ability to service loans. The RBI then stepped in to provide scope for restructuring of advances so that banks had more comfort. This process was still on when the lockdown happened. Now expecting banks to lend more to these enterprises would be expecting too much from them. Besides with the moratorium being in place SMEs were one set of borrowers who took recourse to this facility. This also meant that banks would be hesitant to lend more to them when their servicing ability was limited.

This is where the economic package made a difference. One of the announcements made was that a package of ₹ 3 lakh crore of loans to the SMEs would be guaranteed without any condition by the government which meant that banks could lend to them without fear of defaults as the government would step in. This framework was time bound and the interest rate also fixed to give the two sides comfort. This can be considered to be a very positive move for the SMEs as the hesitancy factor of banks has been addressed.

The 100% collateral-free MSME loan was called the Emergency Credit Line Guarantee Scheme (ECLGS), which was provided by the National Credit Guarantee Trustee Company (NCGTC) to banks, NBFCs and Financial Institutions (FIs). According to this scheme, every eligible MSME or business enterprise can get a pre-approved sanction limit of up to 20% of loan outstanding as on 29 February 2020. This is in the form of additional working capital term loan facility (in case of banks and financial institutions), and additional term loan facility (in case of NBFCs). This is a special scheme to help small businesses battling the economic impact of Covid-19 and includes Pradhan Mantri MUDRA Yojana (PMMY) borrowers.

The loan under this scheme was extended for a period of four years from the date of disbursement and there would be no prepayment charge if a borrower wants to repay early. There would also be no processing fee for such loans. What is important to note is that a there would be a moratorium of one year on the principal repayment, but interest payment would continue during this period. The principal repayment was then be converted into equated installments spread across the remaining period, which is 36 months. A separate loan account was to be opened, which is distinct from the current loan accounts.

Business enterprises or MSMEs that have a combined outstanding loans across different banks, NBFCs and FIs up to ₹ 25 crore as on 29 February 2020, and with annual turnover of up to ₹ 100 crore for FY 2019-20 were eligible for the scheme. Proprietorship, partnership, registered company, trusts and Limited Liability Partnerships (LLPs) were all eligible under the scheme, but only the loans taken for the business was being covered. Any loan taken by a promoter or director in his personal capacity would not be covered under the scheme. What is important to note is that the scheme was valid only for existing customers of a bank, NBFC or FI. This means this scheme was not for new borrowers. Also, the loan account was to be less than or equal to 60 days past due as on 29 February 2020 and the borrower was not been classified as Special Mention Account 2 (SMA 2) or NPA by any of the lender as on 29 February 2020. A borrower must also be registered under GST, unless the business is not required or exempted.

To ensure that the scheme is beneficial to the borrowers and the cost of borrowing is kept low banks or the lending institution had to link their lending rate to one of the external benchmark rates prescribed by RBI plus 1% subject to a maximum of 9.25% per annum. Similarly, NBFCs could not charge more than 14% as interest for the loans under this scheme. This facility was available for borrower from May 23, 2020 to 31 October 2020, or till an amount of ₹ 3 lakh crore has been sanctioned, whichever is earlier.

However, given the time limitation of October meant that the time period was not very long to help to bring about growth. The present exigency is one of survival which means that the funds would be used to tide over the immediate problems that confront them. It should be remembered that at the time of the package announcements, most of these units were non-operational which meant that the window would be effective only for those which were in a state of working with minimum capacity utilization. Also, the package was providing a guarantee and was not free money. Hence, the borrower had to repay the loan at some point of time and taking loans means increasing indebtedness of the entity.

As with all these schemes, the result will be known only after a year or so. The immediate response was said to be good as per the Finance Minister (FM), though there is admittedly more time till October for this to work. The tracking of repayments is critical here which will validate the effectiveness of the guarantee. These loans are likely to be tested only post the moratorium being given on these loans end and hence the jury will really be out after five years.

The table below gives the incremental credit o/s to the MSEs compared with March-end.

Incremental Credit	₹ crore
April	–48,560
May	–71,646
June	–67,003
July	–48,816
August	–44,890
September	–22,284
October	–24,068
November	–48,560

Source: RBI

The table presents some interesting observations. The incremental credit over March has been negative all through the period while the government has made an announcement periodically that the volume of sanctions has been increasing and that it crossed ₹ 2 lakh crore by November beginning. The fact that sanctions and disbursements have been increasing is significant. However, if outstanding credit to the SMEs has come down, it signifies that the new loans have been taken for repaying old loans which is a win-win situation. The bank is happy to get back the earlier loans which protects their quality of assets. The SME is able to repay the loan with a new loan which costs less as the rate has been fixed. The bank is again comfortable with this arrangement as the new loan has been guaranteed by the government.

Therefore, the ECLGS has been effective largely for providing relief to the SMEs to the extent that they are covered by the scheme. A gap has been that firms which did not have borrowings from the system would be left out. This is something which could have also been included as the scheme covered those units which had outstanding performing loans as of February 29th. It can be said that only a limited part of this finance would have been used for growth purposes.

As was expected the scheme was extended further to March 2021, but the interesting observation is that the total sanctions under this scheme for the SMEs had not changed much since November and remained at ₹ 2 lakh crore. The coverage was also widened further in November by the FM to companies with dues of ₹ 50-500 crore and in the list of 26 sectors that were recommended by the K.V. Kamath Committee for one-time restructuring. This would help to cover the balance funding that would be guaranteed of around ₹ 1 lakh crore as the scheme was for ₹ 3 lakh crore.

A conclusion here is that while government can address supply side issues, the demand side is also important and units with less activity and uncertain future would be less inclined to borrow. The attraction here in this scheme was the interest rate which is capped at 9.25% which can be used to repay older loans and hence save on interest cost. It would take some more time before they would be in a position to grow in a meaningful manner.

Chapter 9
Investment Collapses

Capital is that part of wealth which is devoted to obtaining further wealth.

—Alfred Marshall

New investments reckoned during the first quarter of the year came down to a low of ₹ 82,880 crore which is an all-time quarterly number. Since 2005, the average quarterly new investment reckoned has been in the region of ₹ 3-4 lakh crore and hence is indicative of how the lockdown impacted investment decisions.

The lockdown and the uncertainty of its tenure and the implications for other related sectors came in the way of such decisions. The issue was uncertainty about the length of the lockdown. As production stalled in the first quarter there was deferment of investment. Even after the unlock policy was announced, the production levels remained sub-normal which came in the way of new investment decisions. The table below shows that even as late as December, corporate India was cautious in such decisions and hence for the nine months period, just ₹ 2.75 lakh crore was announced which is the lowest in over a decade. In 2013, the levels were less than ₹ 10 lakh crore but were still higher at ₹ 7.75 lakh crore.

New investments announced

	₹ crore
Jun-16	5,43,450
Sep-16	4,30,838
Dec-16	3,31,927
Mar-17	5,43,143
Jun-17	3,36,464
Sep-17	2,70,156
Dec-17	3,72,561
Mar-18	5,50,636
Jun-18	4,70,770
Sep-18	3,09,499
Dec-18	3,37,277
Mar-19	3,68,066
Jun-19	1,58,822
Sep-19	3,41,712
Dec-19	7,01,427
Mar-20	3,79,618
Jun-20	82,880
Sep-20	1,04,806
Dec-20	87,209

Source: CMIE (as of January 2021). Figures could get revised and hence latest numbers could be marginally different.

Since 2017-18, the average quarterly investment announced has tended to be above ₹ 3 lakh crore and was lower than the previous years where the average was above ₹ 4 lakh crore. Hence, there has been a slowdown in the investment cycle in the country in the last few years which got exacerbated in the FY21 due to the lockdown. Investment decisions are based on requirements for the future which means that post lockdown the confidence levels are low.

These investments have been concentrated in a handful of sectors as shown in the table below.

Shares of Sectors in Total (%)

Chemicals and chemical products	14.2
Machinery	5.9
Transport equipment	7.7
Metals	6.5
Electricity	24.3
Transport services	8.1
Information technology	10.1
Construction and real estate	5.1

Source: CMIE

Here it should also be pointed out that these numbers refer to intentions and not actual investment. Such decisions translate into investment over a period of time and hence are at best broadly indicative of the climate and may not materialize.

Also given that there is surplus capacity in most industries with the RBI data on capacity utilization being at a low of 47.3% in June after 69.9% in March 2020. There were signs post September that there was recovery in these utilization rates in certain sectors like steel which was good. For sure these numbers will improve over time. But the loss for the first six months will definitely be a loss or cost for the economy.

Two things stand out here. The first is that it will not be possible for such investment to be compensated for in the coming quarters. As can be seen the first half had investments of ₹ 1.87 lakh crore announced compared with ₹ 5 lakh crore in 2019 and ₹ 7.80 lakh crore in 2018. Normally, private investment trails government capex. Now government capex up to October was ₹ 1.97 lakh crore, a tad lower than that of last year. But up to September, it was lower by almost ₹ 22,000 cr. Hence, while there has been some momentum from the government there would be time lags before private investment picked up pace.

Also, data from the banking sector shows little pick up in credit till November. Growth in bank credit to industry was –5.2% between April and November. It was positive for medium industry at 17% and negative for micro and small and large industry. Quite clearly, there is an issue on both demand and supply sides. On the demand side, fewer companies would be getting in with any speed for fresh investment as the future of lockdowns is still unknown. Probably, till a vaccine is effectively administered, investment levels would be slow and hence take time to revert to the pre-covid levels. It is also true that everyone in business will try their best to get back to normal as soon as possible and hence from the macro standpoint would work towards getting back on track. The question lingering is that while there can be compensations in investment over the next few years, have we lost time for growth? This leads to the other thought.

Second is that the implications for future growth are not positive as investment has a direct bearing on the future growth prospects. Capital investment is a very critical mass which helps to bring about sustained growth and any delay in getting back on track would delay the process of growth. Therefore, the concern of investment falling this year is more from the point of view of the accelerator working slower in terms of contributing to growth. Hence, while investment will pick up over time as the economy has surely started moving along post June, the lags in investment will prolong the process of conversion to final output and hence economic growth.

This may not really strike hard because with GDP growth quite certainly to be a double-digit or high single digit number in FY22, the loss of growth impetus due to lower investment will be forgotten and camouflaged by an apparently better performance. We have been talking of creating a $ 5 trillion economy by 2023. This will mean a longer waiting time as the bridge to this goal gets longer. The GDP size is ₹ 195 lakh crore as of FY21. A $ 5 trillion economy which is equivalent to around ₹ 370-375 lakh crore will require another four-five years of consistent growth of 15% in nominal GDP. This will be a tall order.

Chapter 10
PMI Dithers

Pessimism, when you get used to it,
is just as agreeable as optimism.

—Arnold Bennett

One early indicator of how the economy is faring is the Purchasing Manager's Index (PMI) which is a quick indicator of how manufacturing or services is performing. The beauty of this concept is that it is made available at the beginning of the month for the previous month. It is based on responses to a sample of 500 companies which are asked some basic questions. The PMI dataset features a headline number, which indicates the overall health of an economy, and sub-indices, which provide insights into other key economic drivers such as GDP, inflation, exports, capacity utilization, employment, and inventories. The answers are a plain Yes or No or no change over the previous month which is then aggregated. If the number is above 50 there is an improvement and anything less than 50 means that most are in the negative terrain and output has fallen.

The table below gives the movement in the PMI which are actual responses from industry. Unlike other growth indicators which are reckoned on a year on year basis and susceptible to statistical biases, the PMI is more straight forward and gets the majority view of improvements or status quo or deterioration compared with the previous month. This suits the purpose of analysis here as the answer to the questions would relate April over March which is when the lockdown was most severe. The table below shows how the PMI for manufacturing declined in all the three months following the lockdown being less than 50. In case of services it was even more severe because at 5.4 in April indicated that almost all the respondents said they were worse off. And this refers to companies which would be the larger ones as they are the ones which really drive the overall production numbers in both these segments. Therefore, the damage caused by the shutdown was quite sharp for three months for sure. The consolation is that in May and June the number improved, even though it was less than 50. This was so as there were some signs of loosening of controls over economic activity which got reflected in these numbers.

Month	IHS Markit India manufacturing PMI	IHS Markit India services PMI	IHS Markit India composite PMI
Jan-19	53.9	52.2	53.6
Feb-19	54.3	52.5	53.8
Mar-19	52.6	52	52.7
Apr-19	51.8	51	51.7
May-19	52.7	50.2	51.7
Jun-19	52.1	49.6	50.8
Jul-19	52.5	53.8	53.9
Aug-19	51.4	52.4	52.6
Sep-19	51.4	48.7	49.8
Oct-19	50.6	49.2	49.6
Nov-19	51.2	52.7	52.7
Dec-19	52.7	53.3	53.7
Jan-20	55.3	55.5	56.3
Feb-20	54.5	57.5	57.6
Mar-20	51.8	49.3	50.6
Apr-20	27.4	5.4	7.2
May-20	30.8	12.6	14.8
Jun-20	47.2	33.7	37.8
Jul-20	46.0	34.2	37.2

Month	IHS Markit India manufacturing PMI	IHS Markit India services PMI	IHS Markit India composite PMI
Aug-20	52.0	41.8	46.0
Sept-20	56.8	49.8	54.6
Oct-20	58.9	54.1	58.0
Nov-20	56.3	53.7	56.3
Dec-20	56.4	52.3	54.9

Source: CMIE

May too was very unfavorable for services as the number was at 12.6. The interesting thing here is that for manufacturing the number is approaching 50 as this was the time when all curbs were removed from manufacturing in June for production of essential and non-essential goods. The negative view can be attributed more to the physical challenges of getting the act of production and distribution together.

The PMIs from June onwards have started showing an improvement which went along with the unlock measures of the government. The unlocking has been in different stages which started in June and continued till October. A pause was witnessed in November where the government decided to let the rules which held in October prevail in this month ostensibly to play cautious with the possible spread of the pandemic in the festival season.

As the PMI is a questionnaire-based survey of enterprises which poses questions on whether the company was better off or not on an attribute relative to the previous month it could be expected that companies would reply progressively more in the affirmative as the unlock process was in progress.

The PMI for manufacturing was in the negative territory for four months starting April till July while that for services was in this area for six months till September. October was a turning point where both the indices were in the positive zone.

What does this Mean?

As is evident from other indicators took, the first half of the year was a dampener on account of the lockdown where business levels were lower. Post September, from October onwards there was positivity seen in these indices meaning thereby that they were above 50 and business in general felt that they were better off than the previous month. This is a positive even though overall growth was still truncated in various sectors. But at least sequentially the economy seemed to be on the right path. The cost of the lockdown hence was at least six months for services and four months for manufacturing.

Chapter 11
Inflation Rises

Inflation is as violent as a mugger,
as frightening as an armed robber and
as deadly as a hit man.

—Ronald Reagan

The rabi harvest of 2020 was declared to be very good and this came on top of a good kharif harvest in 2019. Hence, the price effects were to be positive in the sense of inflation being under check on this score. However, with the lockdown coming in the last week of March there were disruptions in the supplies of farm products which had an adverse impact on inflation. Let us see how this transpired.

Several mandis had to restrict their activity on account of the lockdown depending on the severity of the rules laid down by the State Governments. This manifested in the form of restricted timings which affected normal activity. Second, farmers had a challenge getting their stocks to the mandi for sale as movement of people was checked. While theoretically agricultural markets were exempted, the roads to the mandis were patrolled and farmers pushed back in some regions. Third, farmers also had a problem in getting transport facilities which are basically tractors and trucks as they were off the road and the drivers were missing. Fourth, labour to load and unload the stocks was another challenge for the mandis which became barriers to trading. Fifth, the other important participant in a trade, buyer was missing on several occasions. The same problems which afflicted farmers in a smaller manner got magnified at the buyers' end where movement was restricted leading to distortions in the supply chains.

Processors who would normally have bought their material from mandis were not in a position to buy the raw materials as they were not sure of operations of their mills which could be flour or edible oil as their activity was constrained due to the curfews. They also had the same issues as farmers when the grains/oilseeds bought had to cross borders besides finding it hard to get labour for loading/unloading/carriage in trucks. In fact, their supplies would come from vehicles which were stopped at the borders and fined for being on the roads. Further, the labour problem got in the way of running their machines in their factories as a result of which they were unable to process their raw produce. This added pressure in the market and prices went up.

Hence, the lockdown-affected agricultural products, even though output was normal, if not very good. Supply disruptions, absence of manpower, inter-state restrictions added to problems on both demand and supply which affected prices. Therefore, food prices tended to remain high. Also, at the retail end, consumers paid very high prices for food items including vegetables, fruits, cereals, and pulses as supplies got thwarted for the reasons stated above. Given that in cities, farm produces move at least two-three layers before reaching the household, disruption possibilities for these reasons were high at each level. Further, in the months of April-July any infected person in a mandi meant mandatory closure for a certain period of time which could be two to seven days depending on the local jurisdiction rules and regulations. The restriction in timings of shops added to the demand-supply mismatches which led to queuing and increased prices.

The movement in the CPI index from January onwards has been presented below to give a flavour of how inflation moved across months. As can be seen food inflation has been the highest in the index if one excludes pan, intoxicants, etc. The anomaly was stark especially in urban areas due to the factors mentioned above.

Month	General Index	Food and beverages	Pan, tobacco and intoxicants	Clothing & footwear	Housing	Fuel and light	Miscellaneous
Weight	100	45.86	2.38	6.53	10.07	6.84	28.32
Jan-20	7.6	11.7	3.7	1.9	4.2	3.7	4.8
Feb-20	6.6	9.5	4.1	2.1	4.2	6.4	4.5
Mar-20	5.8	7.8	4.7	2.1	3.7	6.6	4.4
Apr-20	7.2	10.5	5.9	3.5	3.9	2.9	5.4
May-20	6.3	8.4	6.3	3.4	3.7	1.6	5.8
Jun-20	6.2	7.9	11.3	2.7	3.6	0.5	6.1
Jul-20	6.7	8.5	10.5	2.8	3.3	2.7	6.8
Aug-20	6.7	8.3	11.2	2.8	3.1	3.2	7.0
Sep-20	7.3	9.8	10.7	3.0	2.8	2.8	6.9
Oct-20	7.6	10.1	10.6	3.1	3.3	2.1	6.9
Nov-20	6.9	8.9	10.4	3.4	3.2	1.6	7.0
Dec-20	4.6	3.9	10.7	3.5	3.2	3.0	6.6

Source: CSO

As the economy started to open partially, producers of goods and services were able to start their operations. The table below gives the movement in inflation rates for the miscellaneous category which got affected on this score. First health became more expensive as can be seen by the inflation number. The cost of healthcare during the pandemic was erratic and chaotic with private players charging exorbitant rates even as the governments tried to cap the treatment charges. Higher charges combined with increased demand for medicines pushed up prices leading to sustained inflation close to 5%.

Transport and communication inflation looks like an anomaly in a situation where the crude oil price had declined sharply due to excess supplies and absence of storage spaces. The futures prices had turned negative temporarily. The high double digit inflation can be traced to the government which was confronting falling revenues due to the shutdown. In a bid to support the revenue the taxes on fuel products was increased sharply with diesel prices going past that of petrol for a brief while in Delhi. As the economy unlocked people preferred to use their vehicles on account of the precautionary motivation as well as the fact that public transport across the country was only partly restored in most cities and towns. The price of petrol at between ₹ 85-90/litre is comparable to the times when the international price had reached a phenomenal $ 140/barrel as against a price of around $ 40/barrel as of November 2020.

Other components like recreation, amusement, air travel, etc. have also witnessed higher inflation rates. Here the reason has been quite straight forward. As businesses were allowed to open up there was a rule which restricted the capacity utilization rates due to the social distancing norms that had to be adhered to. For example, to begin with airlines were allowed to operate keeping the middle seats unoccupied. This made the journeys uneconomical and hence there was a tendency for fares to be increased. The same has been witnessed in entertainment theatres where the restriction on the number of people that can come for the show has made it necessary to increase prices.

In this kind of an environment, the industry which has made merry is the personal care segment that leveraged the opportunity to make major inroads into the customer's basket. The focus on hygiene was hyped and products that were never used in an Indian household like sanitizers became a mandatory part of the home. Prices of these products had been increased as people made a rush for them leading to substantial increase in inflation on this front.

Month	Total	Household goods and services	Health	Transport and communication	Recreation and amusement	Education, stationery, etc.	Personal care and effects
Weight	28.32	3.8	5.89	8.59	1.68	4.46	3.89
Jan-20	4.8	1.8	4.2	6.2	4.5	3.9	7.2
Feb-20	4.5	1.9	4.2	5.2	4.5	3.9	6.9

Month	Total	Household goods and services	Health	Transport and communication	Recreation and amusement	Education, stationery, etc.	Personal care and effects
Mar-20	4.4	1.8	4.2	4.3	4.4	3.9	8.9
Apr-20	5.4	3.8	2.8	5.9	5.7	5.3	10.7
May-20	5.8	3.8	4.1	6.1	5.5	5.3	10.7
Jun-20	6.1	1.8	4.8	8.4	6.2	2.6	12.9
Jul-20	6.8	2.9	4.8	10.3	3.9	2.9	13.7
Aug-20	7.0	2.9	4.8	11.0	4.1	1.7	14.5
Sep-20	6.9	2.8	4.9	11.5	3.7	2.1	12.4
Oct-20	6.9	2.9	5.2	11.2	4.7	2.1	12.1
Nov-20	7.0	3.0	5.6	11.1	4.5	2.5	12.0
Dec-20	6.6	3.0	6.0	9.3	5.2	2.4	11.7

Source: CSO

Inflation in India is important for two reasons. The first is that it is the variable that is targeted for monetary policy. The MPC has been mandated to target a CPI number of 4% with a band of 2% on either ends. This really means that if inflation is above 6% there is a strong reason to increase interest rates. In fact, the gazette also says that if inflation is higher than 6% for over six months, then the MPC is answerable to the Parliament and must explain the same. All this was waived under these conditions.

The MPC had also taken a different stance this time. As the economy had closed down due to a government order and the economy was not able to function, the decision was taken to lower the repo rate and ensure that excess liquidity was generated in the system to ensure that interest rates came down and remained low. This was to help borrowers to ease their burden of debt servicing. It was also to help those companies which wanted to invest more. Therefore, high inflation did not matter.

The second is that the purchasing power of the middle- and lower-income groups was affected sharply. With inflation being above 6% for four successive months the real income of households came down. This was exacerbated by the fact that the interest rates were lowered. Banks were quick to lower their deposit rates—both savings account as well as term deposits. The last straw was when the government lowered the small savings rate too. This has impacted livelihoods of millions of people. On one hand, the government had increased the NREGA wage by ₹ 20/a day and there were cash transfers under the PM Kisan Scheme. But with food inflation being in the 8% range it was a double whammy for those living on a fixed income.

Hence, the inflationary impact on households can be described as being an unintended consequence of the economic lockdown which affected all the people. First people with no jobs had a challenge for subsistence. Second those who faced pay cuts found it hard to manage ends and the moratorium for loan takers was a big benefit. Third, access to goods was a problem given the restrictions in movement of goods and people. Last, the resulting high inflation eroded a large part of the income thus making living conditions even tougher.

Chapter 12
Corporate Performance: Strange Signals

It's a recession when your neighbor loses his job;
it's a depression when you lose yours.

—Harry Truman

The effects of the lockdown were felt quite sharply on the corporate sector where company performance was affected. It was a kind of double whammy for the corporates because even prior to the lockdown the sector was under stress with sales being under pressure for several sectors due to demand being lack lustre. Further, companies have also been striving hard to beat the issues of NPAs especially those in the infra-related space. It is against this background that the performance of this sector can be viewed.

The table below gives the growth rates in certain important variables for a sample of above 3000 companies sourced from CMIE. The data is for non-financial companies. The financial companies have been excluded as they were operational through the period and were less impacted by the lockdown than those which were involved with the production or delivery of goods and services.

	Mar-19	Jun-19	Sep-19	Mar-20	Jun-20	Sep-20
Net sales	8.0	2.4	–6.7	–9.8	–38.8	–10.3
Total expenses	6.1	2.1	–2.3	–1.4	–34.1	–17.6
Salaries and wages	6.4	8.4	5.7	4.1	–3.5	–1.4
PBDIT	8.8	–3.1	–34.9	–31.8	–47.2	65.4
Interest expenses	8.9	13.4	11.7	17.8	5.7	–3.8
PBT	5.9	–16.5	–72.8	–79.7	–89.6	235.7
Count	**3,345**	**3,352**	**3,329**	**3,229**	**3,220**	**3,163**

Source: CMIE

Now what do these numbers tell us? The growth rates in sales, expenses and profits has been presented here. The three quarters which were affected were the last one of FY20 and the first two of FY21. The September 2019 numbers show that there was stress in the system even in FY20 as companies were facing challenges on the demand side in particular. In fact, as can be seen in the table growth in sales had slowed down form June 2019 onwards to September when it declined. Therefore, the situation was not really satisfactory in 2019 and the negative growth rates seen in June and September come over low or negative growth rates in the previous year which is really alarming.

The March 2020 numbers are significant as this is the time when normally companies tend to scale up operations in a bid to meet targets and this gets reflected in higher growth in sales numbers. But with the lockdown being announced from the last week of March, these plans went awry and hence the objective of meeting sales targets was not achieved for most companies. This got reflected in the decline in growth in sales. In fact, the last time when sales registered a decline was in March 2016. This was carried through to a decline in profits. Hence, the one week of lockdown at the end of the month quite sharply affected companies as the last minute ramp up of production was not possible. Also given that the lockdown was a surprise and there was no certainty of when it would end as there was no clarity anywhere about the next steps when the first stage was imposed, companies had to think even harder of the future.

Q1-FY21 was the first quarter which bore the brunt of the lockdown. With two months of an embargo on production of non-essential goods and a total stoppage of several services, it was tough going for companies as sales declined by almost 40%. This was accompanied by a decline in total expenses too which acted as a buffer. But the significant part was that there was a decline in the salary bill which has been discussed separately in terms of the economies invoked by companies on the labour front. There was a sharp slowdown in growth in interest expenses as there were several measures taken by the RBI (discussed separately) to help companies in times of difficultly.

This was the first time probably in a very long time that the corporate results were quite disastrous as the reason was that most sectors were non-operational for two of the three months. In the manufacturing sector it was only FMCG, food products and pharma which were operational to a certain extent, though there were several issues on the logistics side. Others like power were impacted by most offices and factories closing down which affected demand. All services except online related like IT, banking and finance and e-commerce were virtually stalled. Therefore, it was but natural that there was contraction in sales of a high order. The significant part was the fall in expenses too which was natural as demand for raw materials came down. However, a large part of this was due to the reduction in the salary cost (discussed separately in the book). Hence, the reduction in growth in profits which was negative was controlled to an extent. Interest costs were lower for a combination of reasons which was both lower interest rates as well as fall in credit as units not operating did not have to borrow money as working capital. Also investment had come to a standstill in the private sector.

The Q2 results were a continuation of the trend with the difference being that there was improvement as the unlock process started in June. While services faced several restrictions, manufacturing fared better with most activities being permitted. The challenge however was more on the demand side where companies had to assess how it would pan out especially the 'pent up demand' scenario where it was expected that in several sectors consumers would go in for accelerated purchases to make up for what could not be done in the first three months. This helped to ramp up production with the hope that the third quarter would see a more discernible increase in sales. Also, industries like steel and cement were better off in Q2 as there was some movement witnessed in government capex which was seen in the resumption of road building projects. Further the housing sector was expected to witness an uptick in demand during the festival season which helped these industries.

The curious part of Q2 performance was that while there was considerable degrowth in sales, there was a positive growth in profit due to sharp reduction in costs. While this did help the stock market valuation, it was not the ideal way to grow profits. Interest costs too kept falling due to the decline in investment and production.

Therefore, it can be said that three quarters performance was impacted due to the lockdown. Is this serious or just a setback? In any crisis there is always a U-shaped path followed where the decline is followed by either a flat movement or a sharp recovery making it a V-shaped route. This was natural for such a crisis which was caused simply by a diktat that said that everything had to halt except essential goods and services. The hurt for the corporate sector was due to this simple act of putting off the switch. The recovery is certain, though the path would be contingent on several factors which are hard to conjecture. Statistically, things would look better as all growth rates and levels of activity would look better on negative numbers. But the change in the way in which we conduct our lives and business would have a more lasting effect on the final performance of corporates.

Chapter 13

Fiscal Balances get Hurt without Giving Anything!

What is raised by printing notes is just as much taken from the public as is a beer-duty or an income-tax.

What the Government spends the public pays for.

There is no such thing as an uncovered deficit.

—John Maynard Keynes

One of the biggest casualties of the shutdown was the government. That is in terms of their finances coming under strain to a very large extent due to their actions. Much like demonetization, the shutdown was done without any planning and not much thought had gone into it. Therefore, the outcomes were not considered, or so it appears. Because if it were, then some of the steps taken subsequently would not have been announced.

Let us see how things worked here. The shutdown was announced in the last week of March and was followed by two major announcements made by the government and RBI. The government had a plan to provide relief for ₹ 1.7 lakh crore as relief under what was called the Pradhan Mantri Garib Kalyan Yojana. Food grains to be given to the poor and the quantities were specified and free cooking gas was to be given. Cash transfers were to be made and 87 million farmers were to get ₹ 2000. ₹ 1000 was to be paid to senior citizens as ex-gratia. It was stated that 800 mn people would benefit. The NREGA wage was increased by ₹ 20/day to ₹ 202. The irony however was not lost as there was a tacit admission that there were 800 million people in India who could be called low income or poor.

These benefits were for three months and the cost was reckoned as ₹ 1.7 lakh crore.

This was probably the direct spending of the government over and above what was budgeted as the FM did reiterate that these amounts were not part of the allocations made at the time of the Union Budget. Based on the Budget that was drawn up for FY21, this amount would have added 0.7% GDP to the fiscal deficit assuming all other numbers held—which was not possible. This was followed up by the RBI making an early announcement of the monetary policy which lowered rates and enhanced liquidity flows to the banking system.

The pressure on fiscal balances were known but surfaced with a touch of irony when some of the State Governments in May had announced that sale of liquor would be permitted. Given that the lockdown had caused a lot of hardship to individuals and businesses alike it was surprising that the highest priority was put on opening liquor sales which went with enhanced taxes. Delhi for instance imposed a 70% corona tax on liquor and the first day fetched ₹ 7.65 cr. This was reflective of a deeper malaise.

The shutdown meant that there was virtually no economic activity except in the area of essential items which are dominated by food products. Almost all services were blocked which included airlines, restaurants, tourism, hotels, malls, cinema theatres, vehicle workshops, etc. Foreign trade came to a standstill as all countries were in different stages of shutdowns. Trains stopped moving except for transporting essential goods. Sale of liquor and tobacco perforce came to a stop. While some vehicles were on the road, petrol stations were virtually empty doing little business. This is just a summary background of the economic situation.

In such a situation, the problem was first for individuals who were told that life was essential before livelihood and hence there was need for everyone to sacrifice for the greater good. As usual the migrant problem was one which was met with sympathy and the relief provided was supposed to alleviate their physical state though their quality of life was not considered. It was only when the courts intervened that there was action taken for sending the migrants back to their homes.

However, the biggest collateral damage was caused to the government in terms of their revenue which included every layer—the Centre, State and municipal. This is so because governments run on the basis of revenue garnered through taxes and fees and other levies which are dependent on the way in which the economy functions. If the economy fails, it is but natural that the government will earn less as revenue. This is exactly what had happened which led to the realization that the lockdown was not a viable option in the medium term. Having it for 21 days made sense and extending the same was more done because the government did not know what to do as the number of infected cases just kept increasing. In fact, several corporate heads had posed a question: What are we waiting for? There was frustration with the lockdown because there were extensions being announced without specifying the goal post. This was so because the goal could not be defined as the infection cases were rising quite fast over time as more people were tested. The irony is again not lost that by the time the government had taken a stoical view of things with the thought that we have to learn to live with the virus, the lockdown was eased when the number of cases accelerated. The realization that negative economic growth was not sustainable had led to the conclusion that we need to carry on.

On account of the shutdown, the government got affected on all sides. First with the level of unemployment going up there were fewer people to tax. While it can be argued that these people would not be paying substantial tax, the organized sector as explained elsewhere in the book had resorted to salary cuts which could go up to 30-40%. As higher salaried classes witnessed sharper cuts in their pay, the revenue for the government also came down. The combination of salary cuts and lower headcount meant that there was a lower amount of taxable income.

Second, corporate tax collections came down sharply. This was so as the companies started making losses as production got stalled and costs had to be borne like interest, depreciation, salary, in particular. This led to operating profits turning negative in the first quarter which also meant diminished advance tax payments with final payments being lower for certain. While there was sectoral variation with the banking and financial segments doing better, in general profits moved downwards thus affecting tax collections. For companies which made money in the second quarter the lower tax rate helped them to reduce their tax-outgo which in turn affected the government tax collections.

Third service tax, which now comes under GST, was the major casualty as they were non-operational and hence did not have to pay any tax. Luxury hotels and entertainment-related business were main contributors to the exchequer which got impacted. Services typically were taxed at a lower rate relative to goods in the earlier regime and now were subject to 18% rate. With most services being non-operational collections came down.

Fourth, the general GST collections were impacted as it is now a consumption tax. As citizens had no access to non-essential goods, they bought fewer goods and hence paid less tax on them. Most of the essential goods carried lower tax rates in the area of food products and it was but natural that tax payments came down on this front. Therefore, as people were closeted in their homes and hence could consume a limited array of goods, the mirror image was in lower collection of taxes too.

Fifth, the biggest blow to the Centre and States was on fuel. We had a situation where the people were not allowed to move out of home except where very necessary. Hence, the demand for petrol came down sharply. The consumption in April was 0.97 million tonnes, May 1.8 million tonnes, and June 2.3 million tonnes compared with 2.5, 2.7, and 2.6 million tonnes respectively in 2019. Diesel consumption got impacted as there were fewer trucks on the road. Total consumption was lower for this period at 15.0 million tonnes as against 22.5 million tonnes in the previous year which was a fall by around a third. This was so as most of the drivers had left as their jobs were impacted when restrictions were placed. Passenger cars which use diesel had also stopped plying on the roads. Businesses which were not operational did not have to run their Diesel Generating (DG) sets in their establishments. Taxes on petrol and diesel contribute to around ₹ 5-5.5 lakh crore on an annual basis to the government. This was also a time when the crude oil price in global markets had come down to less than $ 20/barrel. As State taxes are *ad valorem*, their revenue got affected directly along with lower consumption which prompted a response of increasing taxes to protect their revenue. The Central Government too increased the excise duties in stages even as the global crude price reverted to the earlier levels of $ 40/barrel. By June end the retail price of both petrol and diesel had reached ₹ 80/litre in Delhi even as consumption sagged. By December the price had crossed ₹ 90/litre for petrol with the price including the dealer margin being around ₹ 30-32/litre and the balance going as taxes to the Centre and States.

Sixth, foreign trade reduced in volumes as the world went into a shutdown phase in the months of April and May. Lower imports or rather in decline in growth of around 19% in the first three months of the year meant that customs collections too were lower. Customs collections account for around ₹ 1.3-1.4 lakh crore a year and with a decline in imports have tended to perform below expectations. This had already been a problem in the past where the economic slowdown before the pandemic had lowered demand for imports which in turn affected customs collections.

Therefore, on all ends the government's revenue was impacted. An important consequence is that the Centre was challenged as there are statutory transfers to be made to the states as per the Finance Commission strictures. In May the FM announced that the Centre had met its commitments. However, when the overall pool of funds that has to be distributed has come down, the amounts that would go to states would also get impacted. The fact that the Centre met the targets is indicative of the accommodation provided. The Centre had already announced that the gross borrowing programme would be ₹ 4.2 lakh crore higher this year taking the amount to ₹ 12 lakh crore. This higher level one can guess was more due to the fall in revenue rather than increase in expenditure as the economic reforms package did reveal that there was limited fiscal push provided through the Budget. Hence, while the problem of ensuring funds transfer to the States was met through this higher borrowing, it was clearly the result of the shutdown that normal revenue flows were impacted.

The RBI meanwhile had enhanced the WMA limits for the States and Centre to 60% of the level as of March of ₹ 32,225 crore and ₹ 1.20 lakh crore for the first half of the year to ensure that there were no temporary pressures on liquidity.

The curious case for the year was the disinvestment programme of the government which was to be around ₹ 2 lakh crore which included the big ticket of LIC as well as the sale of BPCL and Air India. With the oil industry going through volatile times and uncertainty of prospects as the world will be in a recession where demand will be slack, disinvestment of BPCL looked difficult. The same holds for Air India where the airline industry is downbeat with few signs of normalcy returning for the calendar year for certain. With Air India already being a financially injured player, the dim prospects did not augur well for the disinvestment this year. Therefore, a major shortfall for the government on this score was written even before the shutdown was announced. LIC was probably the best bet which is to garner around half of the ₹ 2 lakh crore target. The government could have gone aggressively here, but given that the stock market was down by over 20% prior to the covid strike in the first quarter, the valuation issues came in the way to begin with. By December the stock market had gained momentum but with government attention being focused more on pandemic related issues, disinvestment took a back seat.

The government also looks at non-tax revenue for raising resources with around ₹ 1.5 lakh crore to come as dividend. While the surpluses of the RBI get automatically transferred to the government by stature, the flow from other PSUs were to be affected. The RBI had announced that for FY20 banks would have to skip paying dividend as there were several windows opened to them by the RBI in terms of liquidity and low cost funds. Besides, provisioning commitments for banks rose even on standard assets which were so classified due to flexibility afforded by the central bank. The other PSUs too would be hard pressed to pay dividend to the government and the ability would hinge on how the sector performed.

In short, there were weak lines on the budgetary numbers even at the time of its presentation. The same have been widened post the shutdown and the shape the economy has taken. The government will be pressurized all the time as the revenue flows will remain uncertain. While it looks likely that some sectors will come close to normalcy by the end of the year, most would be trialing at different levels and hence fiscal balances would be pressurized.

How about the States? The State Governments rely a lot on GST, stamp duty, and fuel taxes for managing their budgets. GST as mentioned earlier was to be the Achilles heel for sure this year as consumption was down for a variety of reasons. Stamp duty is dependent on property deals and with this sector under the weather with the migrant issue being the foremost, there was pressure here too. This is one reason why the States have been flogging the fuel segment for extracting higher revenue.

The Centre had however allowed all States to increase their fiscal deficit ratio to 3.5% from the statutory limit of 3% as put by the FRBM Act. There was scope to go ahead of this too but would be conditional. This was relaxed when the GST imbroglio ensued and tranches of 0.25% were permitted for some States. This along with higher WMA allowances would be a comfort for the States which can hopefully meet their expenditure commitments. However, looking at their past, they normally tend to hold back on capex till the fourth quarter and start spending only when they are sure of the fiscal balances for the year. Capex by both the States and Centre were to be important as they determine to a large extent the investment in the country as private sector was slow to pick up.

An interesting statistical puzzle while looking at fiscal ratios is that the denominator was lower than what was projected at the time of the Budget. It was projected that the nominal GDP would change from ₹ 204 lakh crore in 2019-20 to ₹ 225 lakh crore in 2020-21. The assumption here is that nominal GDP would grow by 10% in nominal terms and the economists' calculators were busy drawing up various combinations of real GDP growth and inflation numbers. A spilt of 6% real GDP and 4% inflation looked reasonable under these conditions.

Now for 2019-20, GDP came in lower at ₹ 194 lakh crore going by the first advance estimates. For FY21 the forecasts varied from –5% to 20% to being with (keeping aside the outliers which go beyond 30%) which came down to a range of 5-10% by December with RBI choosing 7.5%. With inflation being say in the region of around 5%, the best possible scenario could be zero growth in nominal GDP. Hence, for states put together, a 4% deficit ratio on GDP of ₹ 194 lakh crore would be 7.8 lakh crore. The CSO placed nominal GDP at ₹ 195 lakh crore and hence the State deficit would be ₹ 7.8 lakh crore.

Progress of Revenue Collections

		April	May	June	July	August	September	October
Income	2019	39,716	20,840	36,371	31,825	36,748	47,504	31,390
	2020	26,978	8,748	26,397	29,121	26,494	48,751	36,612
Corporate	2019	12,376	-11,250	69,514	17,741	22,785	1,38,161	23,429
	2020	19,514	-2,533	37,231	-488	10,991	85,749	22,271
Customs	2019	13,105	15,124	11,251	12,239	10,312	9,807	-7,379
	2020	3,934	5,633	5,849	8,331	8,555	8,045	**10,172**
GST	2019	46,848	34,557	35,400	24,095	68,545	38,132	37,135
	2020	5,934	18,961	30,152	37,902	32,359	37,171	**42,901**
Excise	2019	-114	17,447	19,618	17,893	21,188	19,898	18,021
	2020	80	10,876	**24,391**	**32,548**	**32,503**	**28,355**	**31,886**

Source: Controller of Accounts

The figures in bold indicate the points of time when the revenue collections in 2020 were higher than that in 2019 in the comparable month. With the exception of excise duties where the increase in rates helped to enhance collections, revenue garnered under other headings exceeded last year in October only with income tax collections reaching this mark in September. Nonetheless, on a cumulative basis collection have been lower this year for all of the headings except excise as is given in the table below.

Cumulative Collections April-December (₹ crore)

Revenue head	2019	2020
Income tax	317,652	297,806
Corporate tax	369,533	312,532
GST	368,838	288,223
Customs	85,154	79,598
Excise collections	153,199	235,993
Gross tax collections	13,83,035	13,38,126

Source: Controller of Accounts

It is true that a decline in tax collections would be transient for just a year and hence can be looked at as an aberration. However, here too it would come in the way to fiscal consolidation as the government will have to work hard over the next couple of years to streamline their finances. The Union Budget for FY22 had targeted moving towards a fiscal deficit number of 4.5% by FY26 and hence the earlier target of 3% seems a long way off.

Chapter 14
The GST Farce

Almost all government policy is wrong...
but frightfully well carried out!

—Sir Humphrey in 'Yes Minster'

It can be said that the lockdown impacted all levels of the government. While the GST issue came to the fore due to the transfers that were involved, there have been cases where local municipal corporations have not been able to pay their employees due to non-collection of dues. Local taxes on shops and establishment could not be paid by the owners affecting their revenue. The same held for public spaces like parking which impacted their earnings. Therefore, in a system where all authorities depend on the public to keep the wheels moving, the lockdown had repercussions. And most of the lost revenue cannot be recouped because while pent up demand can increase consumption for a month or two, sustenance is dependent on the economy fully recovering meaning thereby that enough jobs are created, and income generated.

The tables below give the collections of GST for the government under different components in the last two years to get an idea about how much was the shortfall progressively. October was the month when collections in FY21 were higher than that of last year and this continued in November too. A reason often attributed for this increase is the pent up demand argument where households tended to spend more during the festival season as they were not able to consume the requisite quantity in the first six months.

	GST	CGST	SGST	IGST	Compensation cess
Apr-19	1,13,865	21,163	28,801	54,733	9,168
May-19	1,00,289	17,811	24,462	49,891	8,125
Jun-19	99,938	18,366	25,343	47,772	8,457
Jul-19	1,02,083	17,912	25,008	50,612	8,551
Aug-19	98,203	17,733	24,239	48,958	7,273
Sep-19	91,917	16,630	22,598	45,069	7,620
Oct-19	95,380	17,582	23,674	46,517	7,607
Nov-19	1,03,491	19,592	27,144	49,028	7,727
Dec-19	1,03,184	19,962	26,792	48,099	8,331
Apr-20	32,294	-	-	-	-
May-20	62,009	-	-	-	-
Jun-20	90,917	18,980	23,970	40,302	7,665
Jul-20	87,422	16,147	21,418	42,592	7,265
Aug-20	86,449	15,906	21,064	42,264	7,215
Sep-20	95,480	17,741	23,131	47,484	7,124
Oct-20	1,05,155	19,193	25,411	52,540	8,011
Nov-20	1,04,963	19,189	25,540	51,992	8,242
Dec-20	1,15,174	21,365	27,804	57,426	8,579

Source: Government of India

Up to September, the overall collections of GST was ₹ 4.54 lakh crore as against ₹ 6.06 lakh crore in FY20. Of this shortfall of ₹ 1.5 lakh crore around ₹ 1 lakh crore can be explained as being a virtual permanent loss unless there was going to be major uptick in the second half to compensate for the same. In the next two months there were higher collections of around ₹ 10,000 crore which has reduced this deficit. In FY20 total collections for the year were ₹ 12.2 lakh crore which is approximately ₹ 1 lakh crore per month.

How did the Problem get Escalated?

The lockdown meant halt to economic activity. Producers were not allowed to produce their goods and services and consumers had severe restrictions placed in terms of venturing out of their homes. Those who had access to the ecommerce modes were able to buy their essential goods. But services remained out of the domain for at least six months. Also given the differentiation between essential and non-essential goods, all manufacturers were not allowed to get into operations. And as has been explained in several places even those goods that were allowed to be produced had challenges in terms of getting through the labyrinth of rules in different regions. The end result was that consumption levels fell. This held more in services than physical products as the former involved social interaction that was not permitted.

Hence, hotels, restaurants, cinema halls, theatres, airlines, railways, private buses, were closed to different degrees in different states. Non-essential goods like mobile phones, consumer durables, auto, etc. were on the borderline and production was hard given that showrooms were closed. If the retailers were to sell only essentials, those dealing with durable goods were closed. Hence, the consumption levels were affected. And when consumption gets affected, the tax collections are impacted.

The GST is the big tax reform which integrated all taxes on goods for most products. The idea was that there should be one tax rate (which became five in our system) and be uniform cross the country. Earlier the excise duty was primarily a central tax while the sales tax was imposed by states. There was a differentiation between production site and consumption zone. This was integrated through the GST where a consumption tax is imposed at different rates depending on the kind of good or service. The problems began for the government with the lockdown as people could not consume all goods and services. Most of the essential goods had zero or low GST rates of 5%. Also given that several families were in transition and dependent on the free food and income transfer from the government there was little money left to be spent on items beyond the food basket. This impacted the GST collections of both the Centre and State.

The way the GST is structured is that there is a Central GST and State GST which is distributed to ensure equity. Further there was a promise made to all the states when they signed up to be a part of the GST that their revenues would be protected at the rate of 14% per annum. The way it worked was that it was decided that tax revenue on goods and services for States had grown at an average of 14% in the past and hence would be protected at this rate in the future five years. This meant that if their revenues fell short of this mark, the Centre would compensate them for the same. In this context, a compensation cess was created that was to be used to pay the States in case there was a shortfall. But what if all the States had a shortfall at the same point of time?

Such a situation could not have been conceived and as was explained by the FM was 'an act of God'. This was the strange case where GST collections as a whole collapsed for both the Centre and States. The Centre was not in a position to compensate the States as the compensation cess fund did not have the money as collections fell. When the fund was created, it was never expected that there could be such a contingency where all States fell short of revenue at the same time and that the Centre would also be in a similar position. Interestingly, in case the GST was not there, States would have anyway lost this revenue and would not have had any place to turn to as the earlier regime did not provide for such compensation. Therefore, the argument of this situation being an act of God was well placed as it was a very extraordinary situation which probably may never take place in future.

The States did not want to borrow the shortfall as this would add to their borrowing and debt servicing costs. Further, their cost of borrowing would be higher than that of the Centre as typically states pay 40-60 bps higher on their market borrowings relative to the Centre. Besides the borrowers would have to add this amount to their debt which would distort their debt ratios. While the Centre was willing to exempt the fiscal deficit target of 3% under FRBM for this year just like it was done for States which signed up for the power reforms project of DISCOMs, in November 2015, States did not want to take it up and face the task of servicing the same. In fact, the servicing of such debt by States would have anyway been through future flows into the compensation cess fund. The intransigence of States could hence be argued as being politically motivated as the opposition states were not willing to take it up.

The Centre on its part was not willing to do the borrowing. There was a catch in the GST compensation formula. The Centre could compensate the States from the fund provided money was there. If there was no money, the law did not speak of the Centre having to finance the same from other sources. The law was silent as it could never have been expected that such a situation would arise. Now that it had surfaced, the Centre tried to drag its feet on the compensation.

The Centre drew up a plan comprising alternative escape routes. The States would fall short by ₹ 97,000 crore due to the compensation from GST. Also due to the pandemic the calculation was that the States would have a shortfall of ₹ 2.35 lakh crore for the year. The offer made was for the States to sign up and agree such that ₹ 97,000 would be provided through a route carved by the government through the RBI or alternatively they could borrow the entire ₹ 2.35 lakh crore from the market with forgiveness on the FRBM norms. As has been the case with the NDA Government reforms, the States ruled by their constituents were willing while the opposition took a recalcitrant stance.

Hence, there was chasm between the two layers of government which became fairly acrimonious. Finally, the Centre did extend the olive branch by taking on the onus of borrowing ₹ 1.22 lakh crore and compensating the States. This borrowing was not defined as being fresh borrowings and the implication was that it would be paid from within the gross borrowing programme that was announced at ₹ 12 lakh crore. Subsequently, it was made known that the ₹ 1.1 lakh crore of additional borrowing would also be part of the government borrowing programme.

The opposition-run State Governments had finally come round to agreeing to this new engagement and hence the debate was settled. The money would be borrowed by the Centre and passed to the States. This would show as transfers from the Centre which had to be serviced from future earnings in the 'compensation cess' fund both in terms of interest as well as principal. Therefore, it was a win-win situation where there would be a combination of accounting with future payouts in terms of servicing that would pay for this loss.

Policy Approach

Chapter 15

The Grand Design or an Apology for Stimulus

There are no beautiful surfaces without a terrible depth

—Frederic Nietzsche

12th May was important for the nation as the PM announced the extension of the lockdown but also gave an assurance of a ₹ 20 lakh crore of economic package to revive the economy. This was big news and the stock markets woke up with a bang as the Sensex ended 637 points higher on the 13th. The economic package had all elements of a suspense drama as the FM announced various measures in five tranches explaining each time the efforts put in by the government to sustain the economy and the announcements to propel the same. The question on everyone's mind was on the number of ₹ 20 lakh crore of package. Analysts were keen to know how the money would be mobilized as most countries which spoke of a stimulus combined tax cuts with targeted expenditures. Almost every section of the economy waited eagerly to hear what was to be offered and as it was over five tranches it was assumed that everyone would get something at the end of the day.

Here there were great expectations of a fiscal boost by the government as the knowledge that industrial production was negative in April with the PMI for services also coming down to a low of five direct intervention from the government was naturally expected. Also given that the FM had said that the announcements would be in tranches meant that business waited with bated breath each time it was known that there was a package to be announced. These announcements came from 13 to 17th of May with the FM putting the numbers that summed to ₹ 20 lakh crore on the last day. But there were no tax cuts for either individuals or corporates and the package was a mix of reforms and some direct relief for the distressed people.

These packages were structured and looked at specific sectors each time. With a touch of nationalism, the package was presented under the umbrella of Atma Nirbhar Bharat Abiyan which was a continuation of the earlier motto of 'Make in India'. This term did catch attention and led to debate on whether this meant we should stop importing goods at the extreme, and hence similar to the Make in India debate which was based on export promotion or import substitution. In fact, the debate on Make in India has not been resolved as it has been argued both ways—import substitution and export promotion. In case of Atma Nirbhar approach, it was clarified that the idea was to make India a strong economic power and that there was no direct hint at keeping imports out. This rhetoric was however not lost on critics.

Some of the measures in the various tranches announced were the following:

1. ₹ 3 lakh crore Emergency Working Capital Facility for Businesses, including MSMEs. To provide relief to the business, additional working capital finance of 20% of the outstanding credit as on 29 February 2020, in the form of a Term Loan at a concessional rate of interest will be provided. This will be available to units with up to ₹ 25 crore outstanding and turnover of up to ₹ 100 crore whose accounts are standard. The units will not have to provide any guarantee or collateral of their own. The amount will be 100% guaranteed by the Government of India providing a total liquidity of ₹ 3 lakh crores to more than 45 lakh MSMEs. *This was an affirmative step taken by the government as the major hurdle to lending to SMEs was the risk factor. With the government pitching in and providing a guarantee there was a risk mitigation process in place which*

would enable banks to lend to this sector. Banks would otherwise have been wary of lending to this segment.

2. ₹ 20,000 crore Subordinate Debt for Stressed MSMEs. Provision made for ₹ 20,000 crore subordinate debt for two lakh MSMEs which are NPA or are stressed. Government will support them with ₹ 4,000 crore to Credit Guarantee Trust for Micro and Small Enterprises (CGTMSEs). Banks are expected to provide the subordinate-debt to promoters of such MSMEs equal to 15% of his existing stake in the unit subject to a maximum of ₹ 75 lakh. *This was again a positive step that was announced for MSMEs that were distressed.*
3. ₹ 50,000 crore equity infusion through MSME Fund of Funds. Government to set up a Fund of Funds with a corpus of ₹ 10,000 crore that will provide equity funding support for MSMEs. The Fund of Funds shall be operated through a mother and a few daughter funds. It is expected that with leverage of 1:4 at the level of daughter funds, the Fund of Funds will be able to mobilise equity of about ₹ 50,000 crores. *This was a measure meant for the well-performing units that would be supported with funds to an extent from the government which would enable them to raise five times equity in the market. This was an adept mode of financial engineering where the government would put in ₹ 10,000 crore that would enable them to raise multiple times the amount. But a lot would depend on how many units really qualified for such funding and were able to access the equity market at a time when the economy was moribund. Nine months down the line not much was heard on this measure.*
4. Operational measures included those which cleared the business environment rather than any direct aid from the government.
   (i) New definition of MSME. Definition of MSME to be revised by raising the investment limit. An additional criterion of turnover was also being introduced. The

distinction between manufacturing and service sector was also be eliminated.

(ii) Other Measures for MSME. e-market linkage for MSMEs will be promoted to act as a replacement for trade fairs and exhibitions. MSME receivables from government and CPSEs will be released in 45 days.

(iii) No global tenders for government tenders of up to ₹ 200 crore. General Financial Rules (GFR) of the government will be amended to disallow global tender enquiries in procurement of Goods and Services of value of less than ₹ 200 crore.

5. At the individual level there were measures relating to provident funds. These did give some relief for the persons covered, though some measures only allowed for more liquidity to individuals in terms of less contribution to EPF. Given that the contributions are not very significant at most levels such a measure would have helped those who were operating with a lower salary on account of the lockdown with their disposable income going up. The mirror image would be that the government would be saving on paying interest on these funds for three months.

(i) Employees Provident Fund Support for business and organised workers. The scheme introduced as part of Pradhan Mantri Garib Kalyan Package (PMGKP) under which Government of India contributes 12% of salary each on behalf of both employer and employee to EPF will be extended by another three months for salary months of June, July, and August 2020. Total benefits accrued is about ₹ 2500 crore to 72.22 lakh employees.

(ii) EPF contribution to be reduced for Employers and Employees for three months.

(iii) Statutory PF contribution of both employer and employee reduced to 10% each from existing 12% each for all establishments covered by EPFO for next three months. This will provide liquidity of about ₹ 2250 crore per month.

6. ₹ 30,000 crores Special Liquidity Scheme for NBFC/HFC/MFIs. Government will launch ₹ 30,000 crore Special Liquidity Scheme, with liquidity being provided by RBI. Investment will be made in primary and secondary market transactions in investment grade debt paper of NBFCs, HFCs, and MFIs. This will be 100% guaranteed by the Government of India. *This measure was needed as the sector had gone through traumatic times and had the last minute connectivity to borrowers in different parts of the country.*
7. ₹ 45,000 crores Partial Credit Guarantee Scheme 2.0 for Liabilities of NBFCs/MFIs. Existing Partial Credit Guarantee scheme is being revamped and now will be extended to cover the borrowings of lower-rated NBFCs, HFCs and other Micro Finance Institutions (MFIs). Government of India will provide 20% first loss sovereign guarantee to Public Sector Banks. *This would be a contingent liability for the government and in case a loan given by a PSB to any of these institutions failed, the first loss of 20% would be paid by the government. It would not cover the entire loan and the time period for the same was also fixed for two years and not in perpetuity.*
8. ₹ 90,000 crore Liquidity Injection for DISCOMs. Power Finance Corporation and Rural Electrification Corporation will infuse liquidity in the DISCOMS to the extent of ₹ 90000 crore in two equal instalments. This amount will be used by DISCOMS to pay their dues to Transmission and Generation companies. Further, CPSE GENCOs will give a rebate to DISCOMS on the condition that the same is passed on to the final consumers as a relief towards their fixed charges. *This was more in the nature of reforms in the power sector that would make the state electricity companies steady and was not a direct benefit as such. By September the Parliament was informed that over ₹ 70,000 crore was sanctioned to the DISCOMs.*

9. Relief to Real Estate Projects. State Governments are being advised to invoke the Force Majeure clause under RERA. The registration and completion date for all registered projects will be extended up to six months and may be further extended by another three months based on the State's situation. Various statutory compliances under RERA will also be extended concurrently.
10. Tax Relief to Business. The pending income tax refunds to charitable trusts and non-corporate businesses and professions including proprietorship, partnership and LLPs and cooperative shall be issued immediately. *This may be considered to be more of an administrative issue which gives business their dues on time.*
11. Free food grains supply to migrants for two months. For the migrant labour, additional food grain to all the States/UTs at the rate of 5 kg per migrant labourer and 1 kg Chana per family per month for two months, i.e. May and June 2020 free of cost shall be allocated. Migrant labourers not covered under National Food Security Act or without a ration card in the State/UT in which they are stranded at present will be eligible. States/UTs shall be advised to put a mechanism for targeted distribution as envisaged in the scheme. Eight lakh MT of food grain and 50,000 MT of Chana shall be allocated. The entire outlay of ₹ 3500 crore will be borne by Government of India. *The crux of success of such a measure is in ensuring that this benefit reaches the targeted beneficiaries.*
12. Technology system to be used enabling Migrants to access PDS (Ration) from any Fair Price Shops in India by March 2021—One Nation One Ration Card.
13. Scheme for Affordable Rental Housing Complexes for Migrant Workers and Urban Poor to be launched.
14. 2% Interest Subvention for 12 months for Shishu MUDRA loanees—relief of ₹ 1,500 crore. Government of India will provide interest subvention of 2% for prompt payees for a period of 12 months to MUDRA

Shishu loanees, who have loans below ₹ 50,000. The current portfolio of MUDRA Shishu loans is around ₹ 1.62 lakh crore. *This will provide relief of about ₹ 1,500 crore to Shishu MUDRA loanee.*

15. ₹ 5,000 crore credit facility for street vendors. *Identification and delivery of credit is critical here. Banks have reported on occasions that it has become tough to track such borrowers and hence were reluctant to lend to this segment due to fear of default. The main problem here is of identification of the vendors as only those who are registered with the authority can get such loans. Further, providing a loan without allowing them to operate makes it hard for them to service the loans. This also is a concern for the bank as the loan comes without collateral.*

16. ₹ 70,000 crore boost to housing sector and middle income group through extension of Credit Linked Subsidy Scheme for MIG under PMAY (Urban). The Credit Linked Subsidy Scheme for Middle Income Group (annual income between ₹ 6 and 18 lakh) will be extended up to March 2021. This will benefit 2.5 lakh middle income families during 2020-21 and will lead to investment of over ₹ 70,000 crore in housing sector. This will create significant number of jobs by giving boost to Housing sector and will stimulate demand for steel, cement, transport and other construction materials. *This was an extension of an existing scheme and the success would depend on access to potential borrowers.*

17. ₹ 6,000 crore for creating employment using CAMPA funds. Approximately, ₹ 6,000 crore of funds under Compensatory Afforestation Management & Planning Authority (CAMPA) will be used for Afforestation and Plantation works.

18. ₹ 30,000 crore Additional Emergency Working Capital for farmers through NABARD.

19. ₹ 2 lakh crore credit boost to 2.5 crore farmers under Kisan Credit Card Scheme. *This scheme has been in*

existence for several years now with farmers using the facility on a regular basis.

20. ₹ 1 lakh crore Agri Infrastructure Fund for farm-gate infrastructure for farmers. *Such allocations would admittedly be over a period of time with the right channels being identified by the government.*
21. ₹ 10,000 crore scheme for Formalisation of Micro Food Enterprises (MFE).
22. ₹ 20,000 crore for fisherman through Pradhan Mantri Matsya Sampada Yojana (PMMSY).
23. Animal Husbandry Infrastructure Development Fund—₹ 15,000 crore. An Animal Husbandry Infrastructure Development Fund of ₹ 15,000 crore will be set up, with an aim to support private investment in Dairy Processing, value addition and cattle feed infrastructure. Incentives will be given for establishing plants for export of niche products.
24. Promotion of Herbal Cultivation: Outlay of ₹ 4,000 crore.
25. Beekeeping initiatives—₹ 500 crore.
26. Introduction of Commercial Mining in Coal Sector. The government will introduce competition, transparency and private sector participation in the Coal Sector. *This was launched quite successfully and can be treated as a major step taken to sell coal blocs to private parties. But the reform per se is sector specific and not really in the nature of tackling the pandemic.*
27. Enhancing Self Reliance in Defence Production. *A good objective that will help domestic companies in course of time. Again this would be outside the purview of tackling the pandemic.*
28. Aviation reforms covering various areas. Six more airports have been identified for second round bidding for Operation and Maintenance on Public-Private Partnership (PPP) basis. Additional investment by private players in 12 airports in first and second rounds

is expected to bring around ₹ 13,000 crore. Another six airports will be put out for the third round of bidding. *This measure may be viewed as a medium-term reform for the sector with no impact on the present.*

29. The government will enhance the quantum of Viability Gap Funding (VGF) for social infrastructure up to 30% each of Total Project Cost as VGF by the Centre and State/Statutory Bodies. For other sectors, VGF existing support of 20% each from Government of India and States/Statutory Bodies shall continue. Total outlay is ₹ 8,100 crore. Projects shall be proposed by Central Ministries/State Government/Statutory entities. *This is a medium-term measure which will help over a period of time and is not related to the pandemic.*
30. ₹ 40,000 crore increase in allocation for MGNREGS to provide employment boost. *This is an affirmative action which directly helps labour in the rural areas especially the migrants. NREGS has been a very successful programme over the years and is well established to enable transfer of income to the targeted households. But given that the amount which has been allotted for FY22 is down to ₹ 73,000 crore the number of beneficiaries would tend to be lower this year.*
31. Dircct listing of securities by Indian public companies in permissible foreign jurisdictions. This is a reform which is good from the fund raising part which is otherwise outside the purview of the pandemic relief.
32. Increase borrowing limits of States from 3% to 5% for 2020-21 only and promoting State-level reforms. Centre has decided to increase borrowing limits of States from 3% to 5% for 2020-21 only. This will give States extra resources of ₹ 4.28 lakh crore. Part of the borrowing will be linked to specific reforms (including recommendations of the Finance Commission). Reform linkage will be in four areas: universalisation of 'One Nation One Ration card', Ease of Doing Business, Power distribution and Urban Local Body revenues. A specific

scheme will be notified by Department of Expenditure on the following pattern:

(i) Unconditional increase of 0.50%.

(ii) 1% in four tranches of 0.25%, with each tranche linked to clearly specified, measurable and feasible reform actions.

(iii) Further 0.50% if milestones are achieved in at least three out of four reform areas.

All these measures were announced over a period of five days and there was a lot of expectations of tax cuts and specific relief measures for different sectors. However, as the tranches were announced and the measures analyzed it was clear that the government was keeping in mind the fiscal space and unlike other nations which made several tax cuts and cash transfers, in the Indian case formal obeisance was being paid to the impact on the fiscal deficit. And the last series of announcements had laid down the exact break-up of this ₹ 20 lakh crore of fiscal stimulus that was spoken of by the PM.

Measures announced in March	
Revenue lost due to tax concessions since March 22, 2020	7,800
Pradhan Mantri Garib Kalyan Package (PMGKP)	1,70,000
PM's announcement for Health sector	15,000
Measures in May	
Emergency W/C Facility for Businesses, including MSMEs	3,00,000
Subordinate Debt for Stressed MSMEs	20,000
Fund of Funds for MSME	50,000
EPF Support for Business and Workers	2800
Reduction in EPF rates	6750
Special liquidity Scheme for NBFC/HFC/MFIs	30,000
Partial credit guarantee Scheme 2.0 for Liabilities of NBFCs/MFIs	45,000
Liquidity Injection for DISCOMs	90,000
Reduction in TDS/TCS rates	50,000

Measures announced in March	
Free Food grain Supply to Migrant Workers for two months	3500
Interest Subvention for MUDRA Shishu Loans	1500
Special Credit Facility to Street Vendors	5000
Housing CLSS-MIG	70,000
Additional Emergency Working Capital through NABARD	30,000
Additional credit through KCC	2,00,000
Food Micro enterprises	10,000
Pradhan Mantri Matsya Sampada Yojana	20,000
Operation Greens	500
Agri Infrastructure Fund	1,00,000
Animal Husbandry Infrastructure Development Fund	15,000
Promotion of Herbal Cultivation	4,000
Beekeeping Initiative	500
Viability Gap Funding	8,100
Additional MGNREGS allocation	40,000
Total	**11,02,650**
Earlier Measures incl PMGKP	**1,92,800**
RBI Measures (Actual)	**8,01,603**
Aggregate	**20,97,053**

Source: PIB

It can be seen that the stimulus package which was expected was more in the nature of a medium-term reforms plan that covered all critical sectors. For example, the first three measures announced in May for the SMEs had an amount of ₹ 3.7 lakh crore. But the actual fiscal impact was ₹ 14000 crore only as ₹ 10,000 crore was to be put in the fund of funds and ₹ 4000 paid to the Credit Guarantee Trust of SMEs. The ₹ 75,000 crore facility for NBFCs was only a guarantee or partial credit guarantee being given by the government and did not involve any fiscal outlay being a contingent liability. The ₹ 90,000 crore for DISCOMs was funding by PSUs and not by the government. The PF and TDS allowances were more in nature of deferred payments on tax and higher disposable income for the individuals but did not involve any expense or loss for the government. TDS not being there does not absolve the individual from paying tax which has to finally paid at the end of the year.

Further, the ₹ 2 lakh crore of Kisan credit cards flow of funds was to come from banks as was the ₹ 70,000 crore of funding by NABARD. The housing amount of ₹ 70,000 crore was the potential investment to flow due to the concessions given on the credit-linked subsidy scheme. The Agri infrastructure fund is more of a medium-term nature which has to be provided for in the future Budgets.

Therefore, the entire set of policies were more of enablers of growth with direct focus on relief which came as the food relief programme as well as NREGA which helped the people in distress. This is in continuation of the revealed ideology of the government which works on the premise that the government is an enabler of growth and not an instrument. There is definitely nothing amiss in this approach but it also needs to be understood that when we talk of the ₹ 20 lakh crore of package of the government, a large part is really outside the budget and while 40% came from the RBI which provided liquidity to the system, another 40% was through guarantees given or funds channeled by PSUs including NABARD. Probably around 10-15% were direct spending by the government. Even here it should be remembered that the free food given would be offloading of surplus stocks with the FCI and not fresh purchases by the government. In a way, the surplus stocks have been put to good use.

On June 30th, the PM announced an extension of the free food scheme till the end of November which was the festival season which would cost the government ₹ 90,000 crore. Combined with the ₹ 60,000 crore spent in the first three months, the total fiscal stimulus for the poor would be ₹ 1.5 lakh crore.

The covid impact of lockdown was used as the fulcrum for ushering in a series of reforms. This included the power sector, mining, agriculture, SMEs, infrastructure like airports, etc. The idea was to plug the gaps for various sectors so that doing business became easier. The role of the government has hence been one of enabler which seeks to ensure that business can operate freely. The actual outlay from the package has been limited to providing relief which was actually done in March with some parts being extended in May.

Critics do however point out whether there has been a fiscal stimulus per se here with the government going in for some substantive capex for example or tax cuts which pushes up overall level of spending in the country. The answer is not really as most of the stimulus as can be seen in the table above is in the form of facilitating credit which has been done mainly by the RBI through TLTROs and LTROs and special windows for mutual funds. The government's role has been restricted more to providing guarantees to the loans being given to the SMEs which is a contingent liability and does not really involve a fiscal entry presently. However, to be fair to the government it was never called a fiscal stimulus package but an economic package which logically can cover the monetary sector as well though the fact that the RBI action was taken before this announcement meant that the past also got included in the package. Besides the fact that there were reforms in various sectors meant that the larger picture was kept in mind. The jury is still out on the efficacy of these measures in alleviating the problems of the people.

Any which way none of the measures announced could be less than useful as they were very much required for the development of the requisite sector and was very much on the agenda all the time. It was a different issue that there were expectations of tax cuts along the way for both corporates as well as individuals. This may have been a bit over the top as the corporate tax rate was already cut in FY20 which made it easy on them. Individual tax cuts would have helped.

There are less hopes of a fiscal stimulus package to come up during the course of the year as the revealed preference appears to be one where the government enables growth by removing barriers and substantially enables lending through the financial system. But direct give away to the people has been confined only to providing relief to the needy in terms of income and food. But the approach till May has not gone beyond these frontiers.

The so-called Diwali Bonanza

There was another round of stimulus announced by the FM in October to spur consumption and investment. On the consumption side, there were two proposals for government employees. Some of the excerpts are given below.

Under LTC Cash Voucher Scheme, the government had decided to give cash payment to employees in lieu of one LTC during 2018-21, in which full payment on leave encashment and tax-free payment of LTC fare in three flat-rate slabs depending on class of entitlement would given. An employee, opting for this scheme, will be required to buy goods/services worth three times the fare and one time the leave encashment before 31 March 2021. The items bought should be those attracting GST of 12% or more. Only digital transactions are allowed, GST Invoice to be produced. The estimated cost of LTC Cash Voucher Scheme was estimated to be ₹ 5,675 crore for Central Government employees and ₹ 1,900 crore for PSBs and PSUs. If States and private sector also followed suit the potential increase in consumer demand would be ₹ 28,000 crore.

Second, was a special Festival Advance Scheme which was meant for non-gazetted government employees was being revived as a one-time measure, for gazetted employees too. All central govt. employees can now get interest-free advance of ₹ 10,000, in the form of a prepaid RuPay Card, to be spent by March 31, 2021. The one-time disbursement of Special Festival Advance Scheme is expected to amount to ₹ 4,000 crore. If given by all State Governments, another ₹ 8,000 crore is expected to be disbursed.

On the side of investment, the Centre had given a special interest-free 50-year loan to States is for ₹ 12,000 crore capital expenditure. All the above interest-free loans given to states are to be spent by March 31, 2021; 50% will be given initially, remaining upon utilization of first 50%. Under Part 3 of ₹ 12,000 crore interest-free loans to states, ₹ 2,000 crore will be given to those states which fulfill at least three out of four reforms spelled out in Aatma Nirbhar Bharat package. This is over and above other borrowing ceilings.

Additional budget of ₹ 25,000 crore (in addition to ₹ 4.13 lakh crore given in Budget 2020-21) is being provided for capital expenditure on roads, defence, water supply, urban development, and domestically produced capital equipment.

The measures announced was to boost demand by ₹ 73,000 crore.

Now one can be critical of these measures. In an age of uncertainty would employees like to spend such money? Second, the LTC is a part of the pay and merely allowing the same to be spent on consumer goods is not really a stimulus. Third, the condition that one had to spend three times the LTC amount was a dampener as if a person had a LTC payment of ₹ 1 lakh, spending had to be on ₹ 3 lakh of a good which means that the additional funds had to be financed by the individual. Third, the festival advance is not really very high and has to be repaid and is not free money. Individuals may not really find this of great use especially in the government sector where all jobs and pay cheques were unaffected by this lockdown. The same in the private sector would have helped. While definitely at the margin there could be a push provided to consumption as getting a part of the salary in a larger quantity would help, the overall impact would tend to be limited.

The additional borrowing for capex also deserves some comment. States have been allowed to use such funds for making payments for existing projects. Hence, the incremental investment may be limited. States had run into the problem of financing budgeted capex due to the slowdown in flow of revenue. This move would help to alleviate the same and ensure that projects do not get held back due to paucity of funds. Further the overall amount of ₹ 12,000 crore could be interpreted as being too low as it is being spread across multiple states. While the entire amount would be utilized by states given that the funding is at a zero cost which is repayable after 50 years it cannot lead to bulky investments. The condition that 50% would be given immediately while the rest would be contingent of the progress made in capex was the catch and it will be interesting to see how many states are able to make use of the balance amount of ₹ 6000 crore by the end of the year.

Pre-Diwali the FM came out with what was called Atmanirbhar Bharat-3.0. The package was termed as another stimulus worth ₹ 2.65 lakh crore with the presentation made showing that the total stimulus given by the government which included the RBI contribution was 15% of GDP. However, while the numbers were impressive enough, the reason industry was not too excited was that the package was a combination of liquidity funding through guarantees, medium-term reforms that would work after four-five years and not immediately.

For example, the programme of ₹ 2.65 lakh crore had a production linked incentive (PLI) scheme for ₹ 1.45 lakh crore. The idea was that for the selected ten sectors the government would provide an incentive to units which met a certain criterion in terms of fresh investment made with resulting production. This is to be spread over five years. The scheme per se cannot be contested but has to be classified in the category of medium-term reform as these criteria had to be achieved earmarked to on a base year. Given that FY21 is a low year, no company would qualify for the benefit which would have been a cash payment. Therefore, the response of business was more futuristic.

Similarly, the package had funding for NIIF for ₹ 6000 crore which would help to build an infrastructure funding of ₹ 1 lakh crore over five years. This would be through additional equity participation from sovereign funds and additional debt being raised. The same was with the ₹ 3000 crore for EXIM Bank that was to push exports

The summary of the expenses are given below.

Housing for All - PMAY-U	18,000
Boost for Rural Employment	10,000
R&D Grant for Covid Suraksha—Indian vaccine development	900
Industrial Infrastructure, Industrial Incentives and Domestic Defence Equipment	10,200
Boost for Project Exports—Support for EXIM Bank	3,000
Boost for Atma Nirbhar Manufacturing—Production Linked Incentives	1,45,980

Support for Agriculture—Fertiliser Subsidy	65,000
Boost for Infrastructure—Equity infusion in NIIF Debt PF	6,000
Atma Nirbhar Bharat Rozgar Yojana (overall ₹ 36,000 crore	6,000
Total	**2,65,080**

Source: PIB

The direct expenditures from the above were the ones relating to housing, rural employment, rozgar yojana to the extent of 25% as it was spread over two years, industrial infrastructure and a part of the nebulous amount put for fertilizers subsidy as by November most of sowing for the rabi season was completed and there would have been less demand for the input. One explanation could have been overshooting of the budgeted amount of around ₹ 70,000 crore. But the provision made here did seem to be on the higher side for sure.

It did appear like that the various measures that were announced in May which also took in the policies announced earlier by the government and the RBI were looking at different time periods under the umbrella of Atma Nirbhar Bharat which was a misnomer to an extent. If the idea was to make the economy strong and resilient, then the package had clearly a medium to long-term combination of measures. There were some measures for relief thrown in during this period which was quite divorced from the concept of building a strong and resilient economy in future. This amalgamation of measures had led to various economists and analysts trying to sort out these numbers and gauging what was part of the stimulus of an immediate nature as is normally spoken of and what were reforms measures or even budgetary measures like the one referring to the subsidies.

An interesting omission on November 12th package was that the relief measures of free food which was to last till the end of the month did not find any mention in terms of any extension being given.

The point which is reinforced in all these measures is that the government at the Centre would be more of a facilitator of reforms and schemes. Money spent is being done on a case by case basis and the principle of zero-base budgeting is being followed where every expenditure has to be justified.

What to Make of this Package?

If a stance had to be taken on the power of these measures, it can be said that there were steps taken forward in a limited manner when it came to the immediate requirements which had to go beyond provision of food and cash to the neediest. By not extending the free food programme, the signal given was that the people had to be on their own. The market would decide whether the migrants could go back to work or even find employment if displaced. To this extent, it is a disappointment because ideally more handholding would have been called for this section. For the middle class, there was not much to be had and the struggles during the lockdown which included loss of work or pay cuts, would remain unaddressed. This segment would have to learn to live with the catastrophe of a lockdown with no recourse. Business was shown a lot of funds, but there were caveats everywhere and the large infusion of liquidity may have helped them to an extent but with bond yields coming down, supported the government more than anyone else as banks were wary of lending to lower rated entities. Sector-based reforms were there which will work over a period of time provided the will to see them through remains.

In this context, it is necessary to evaluate what other countries have done in terms of providing a stimulus on the fiscal side. This is discussed in some detail in the next chapter.

Chapter 16

What have Other Countries Done?

Government's first duty is to protect the people, not run their lives.

—Ronald Reagan

The crisis this time was quite unique as it was not a financial one nor was it an economic collapse due to market failure. It was a pure man made crisis which has been engendered by governments all over the world where there appeared to be no alternative to control the spread of the virus and announcing and implementing a lockdown for an unknown time seemed to be the only way out. The economic damage that is caused on human livelihood was unfathomable and the panic chain reaction across countries brought the ball back to the government's court. It was one thing to say that people had to be locked up at home. Only essentials were allowed. This meant that both demand and supply were affected. People could not go out and spend as they were not allowed to do so. People in the capacity of labour could not go to produce goods and services as activity was restricted. Therefore, the calamitous effect was in the form of fall in GDP growth and unemployment.

The table below gives the forecasts of the IMF for growth of different countries at three different points of time. This is indicative of the impact of the pandemic which resulted in a lockdown which in turn affected economic activity.

2020	January	April	June	October	Jan 2021
World	3.3	–3.0	–4.9	–4.4	–3.5
Developed	1.6	–6.1	–8.0	–5.8	–4.9
USA	2.0	–5.9	–8.0	–4.3	–3.4
UK	1.4	–6.5	–10.2	–9.8	–10.0
Euro	1.3	–7.5	–10.2	–8.3	–7.2
Japan	0.7	–5.2	–5.8	–5.3	–5.1
Emerging	4.4	–1.0	–3.0	–3.3	–2.4
China	6.0	1.2	1.0	1.9	2.3
India	5.8	1.9	–4.5	–10.3	–8.0

Source: IMF

As can be seen in the table, with the passage of time there have been significant revisions made in the GDP forecasts of the world economy as well as India. What started off with good optimism before the pandemic struck in March did reach a crescendo in terms of the most pessimistic picture in June. By this time various countries had gotten into the lockdown mode and it was possible to conjecture how the economies would shape up in the year. By October it did appear that most of the Western developed countries were over the lockdown especially in Europe where it was business as usual with normalcy returning. Hence, the estimates were revised again and the direction was positive for most of the developed nations. However, India was in the negative zone as the infection rate had neared the 100,000 per day mark. Also the pace of opening up the economy was slow and gradual and issues like labour and supply chains remained problematic. Therefore, the estimate for India's growth turned very negative at 10.3% which is quite different from the marginally positive number forecasted in April. In fact, the lockdown in India was most stringent and introduced at a time when the infection levels were extremely low to the extent of being non-existent relative to the size of the population. Quite clearly, things did not work out the way it was expected.

Under these conditions governments in most countries took different kinds of action which are enumerated below. This is based on what IMF has reported on their web site. There could hence be additions to the same as over time countries have added or withdrawn various kinds of supports as countries moved towards normalcy. The purpose of presenting this information is to juxtapose what countries did to support their economy with what the Indian government had done.

USA

- $483 billion Paycheck Protection Program and Health Care Enhancement Act. This included $321 billion for additional forgivable Small Business Administration loans and guarantees to help small businesses that retain workers, $62 billion for the Small Business Administration to provide grants and loans to assist small businesses, $75 billion for hospitals and $25 billion for expanding virus testing.
- An estimated $2.3 trillion (around 11% of GDP) Coronavirus Aid, Relief and Economy Security Act ("CARES Act") which included $293 billion to provide one-time tax rebates to individuals, $268 billion to expand unemployment benefits, $25 billion to provide a food safety net for the most vulnerable, $510 billion to prevent corporate bankruptcy by providing loans, guarantees, and backstopping Federal Reserve 13(3) program, $349 billion in forgivable Small Business Administration loans and guarantees to help small businesses that retain workers, $100 billion for hospitals, $150 billion in transfers to state and local governments and $49.9 billion for international assistance.
- $8.3 billion Coronavirus Preparedness and Response Supplemental Appropriations Act and $192 billion Families First Coronavirus Response Act. They together provide around 1% of GDP for Virus testing, development of vaccines, therapeutics, and diagnostics; support for the Centers for Disease Control and Prevention responses. Further two weeks paid sick leave; up to three months emergency leave for those infected (at two-third pay); food assistance; transfers to states to

fund expanded unemployment insurance. $1.25 billion in international assistance. In addition, federal student loan obligations have been suspended for 60 days.

United Kingdom

Tax and spending measures included additional funding for the NHS, public services and charities (£16 billion). Measures to support businesses (£29 billion), including property tax holidays, direct grants for small firms and firms in the most-affected sectors, and compensation for sick pay leave; and strengthening the social safety net to support vulnerable people (by £8 billion) by increasing payments under the Universal Credit scheme as well as expanding other benefits.

The government launched three separate loans schemes to facilitate business' access to credit. Together with the British Business Bank the Coronavirus Business Interruption Loan Scheme to support SMEs and the Coronavirus Large Business Interruption Loans Scheme to support bigger firms, which carry an 80% guarantee for loans up to £5 million for the former and up to £300 million for the latter. In addition, the government had put in place the Bounce Bank Loan Scheme for SMEs with 100% guarantee for loan amounts up to £50,000. It also deferred VAT payments for the second quarter of 2020 until the end of the financial year and income tax payments of the self-employed by six months.

The government was to pay 80% of the earnings of self-employed workers and furloughed employees (to a maximum of £2,500 per employee per month) initially for the period March-May. For furloughed employees, the scheme was extended until end-October. Starting in July employers were allowed to furlough employees for part of the daily working hours. Government coverage was to fall to 70% of wages in September (up to £2,187) and 60% in October (up to £1,875) with employers required to contribute the difference to 80%of wages (up to £2,500). The scheme for the self-employed was extended for three more months but at a reduced level of 70% of earnings.

Trade credit insurance for business-to-business transactions was to receive up to £10 billion of government guarantees through the Trade Credit Reinsurance Scheme, with the scheme available for nine months. The government put in place a £1bn package to support firms driving innovation and development through grants and loans.

China

An estimated RMB 4.2 trillion (or 4.1% of GDP) of discretionary fiscal measures were announced. Key measures included:

- Increased spending on epidemic prevention and control,
- Production of medical equipment,
- Accelerated disbursement of unemployment insurance and extension to migrant workers,
- Tax relief and waived social security contributions, and
- Public investment.

The overall public sector expansion is expected to be significantly higher, reflecting the effect of improvements of the national public health emergency management system, additional support through state-owned enterprises, and automatic stabilizers.

Russia

Key measures included increased compensation for frontline medical staff as well as health and safety inspectors. Further, individuals under quarantine were to receive sick leave benefits and sick leave pay to equal at least the minimum wage until the end of 2020. The standard unemployment benefits were equal to at least the minimum wage for three months, including for sole proprietors. The minimum unemployment benefit was to be tripled until end-July; and eligibility to be extended by three months.

A novel measure was that children up to three years of age were to receive an additional lumpsum benefit for three months, starting in April. All children 3-15 years of age were eligible for a one-time lumpsum benefit. Also all children under 16 years of age were eligible for another one-time lumpsum benefit. These additional lumpsum benefits for each child for up to five months was to cover the case if a parent lose jobs, including for parents who lost their jobs before March 1.

On the other side, interest rate subsidies were given for SMEs and systemically important enterprises. Tax deferrals were provided for most-affected companies on most taxes. Deferrals on social contributions for SMEs in affected sectors was to carry on for six months. Additionally, social contributions by SMEs on wages in excess of the minimum wage permanently reduced and social contributions permanently reduced for IT firms.

A tax holiday on all taxes (excluding VAT) and social contributions for Q2 for SMEs, sole proprietors, and NGOs providing social services was announced. Registered self-employed were to be refunded their taxes for 2019 and get a partial refund on their 2020 taxes. The eligibility age to register as self-employed was lowered from 18 to 16. Sole proprietors were to get a partial refund on their social contributions. There were deferrals on rent payments to all levels of government until the end of the year plus zero rent to the federal government for three months for SMEs in affected sectors. Budget grants for SMEs in affected industries were given to cover salaries at the rate of one minimum salary per employee for two months plus subsidized and forgivable loans for all enterprises in affected industries to pay minimum wages for six months. Zero import duties for pharmaceuticals and medical supplies and equipment were provided for. Subsidies were given to airlines, airports, automakers. Finally, there was an expanded eligibility for subsidized mortgage lending. The total cost of the fiscal package is currently estimated at 3.4% of GDP.

Brazil

To mitigate the impact of COVID-19, the authorities announced a series of fiscal measures adding up to 11% of GDP, of which the direct impact in the 2020 primary deficit is estimated at 6.5% of GDP. Congress declared a state of "public calamity" on March 20, lifting the government's obligation to comply with the primary balance target in 2020. This is something significant that could have been considered in India. The government also invoked the escape clause of the constitutional expenditure ceiling to accommodate exceptional spending needs. Emergency measures were to be included in a separate (so-called 'war') 2020 budget, not bound by the provisions of Brazil's Fiscal Responsibility Law and the constitutional golden rule. The fiscal measures included temporary income support to vulnerable households (bringing forward the 13th pension payment to retirees, expanding the Bolsa Familia program with the inclusion of over one million more beneficiaries, cash transfers to informal and unemployed workers, and advance payments of salary bonuses to low income workers), employment support (partial compensation to workers which are temporarily suspended or have a cut in working hours, as well as temporary tax breaks and credit lines for firms that preserve employment), lower taxes and import levies on essential medical supplies, and new transfers from the Federal to State Governments to support higher health spending and as cushion against the expected fall in revenues. Financial assistance states and municipalities—with a temporary stay of debt payments—was also announced.

Public banks expanded credit lines for businesses and households, with a focus on supporting working capital (credit lines add up to over 4% of GDP), and the government backed about 1% of GDP in credit lines to SMEs and micro-businesses to cover payroll costs, working capital and investment. In India, the SME guarantee support was ₹ 3 lakh crore or 1.5% of GDP which is hence comparable. The National Treasury responded to pressures in the interest rate futures market by announcing a program for the simultaneous auctions (buying and selling) of government securities. This has also been done by the RBI to balance liquidity.

France

France legislated in April an increase in the fiscal envelope devoted to addressing the crisis to €110 billion (nearly 5% of GDP, including liquidity measures), from an initial €45 billion included in an amending budget law introduced in March. This added to an existing package of bank loan guarantees and credit reinsurance schemes of €315 billion (close to 14% of GDP). Key immediate fiscal support measures included:

- streamlining and boosting health insurance for the sick or their caregivers
- increasing spending on health supplies
- liquidity support through postponements of social security and tax payments for companies and accelerated refund of tax credits (e.g. CIT and VAT)
- support for wages of workers under the reduced-hour scheme
- direct financial support (solidarity fund) for affected microenterprises, liberal professions, and independent workers
- postponement of rent and utility payments for affected microenterprises and SMEs
- additional allocation for equity investments or nationalizations of companies in difficulty
- facilitating granting of exceptional bonuses exempt from social security contributions
- extension of expiring unemployment benefits until the end of the lockdown and preservation of rights and benefits under the disability and active solidarity income schemes.

The authorities announced a gradual phasing-out of support measures starting in June, except for industries that still faced opening restrictions (e.g. tourism, which will benefit from targeted exemptions from taxes and social security contributions, and the reduced-hour scheme and the solidarity fund until end-2020). They have also announced additional support plans for the hardest-hit sectors (e.g. incentives to purchase greener vehicles and green investment support for the auto and aerospace sectors). A third budget amendment increasing the fiscal package to €135 billion was also announced.

Italy

On March 17, the government adopted a €25 billion (1.4% of GDP) "Cura Italia" emergency package. It included funds to strengthen the Italian health care system and civil protection

(€3.2 billion), measures to preserve jobs and support income of laid-off workers and self-employed (€10.3 billion), measures to support businesses, including tax deferrals and postponement of utility bill payments in most affected municipalities (€6.4 billion), and measures to support credit supply (€5.1 billion).

In April, the Liquidity Decree allowed for additional state guarantees of up to €400 billion (25% of GDP). The guarantee envelope from this and earlier schemes aimed to unlock more than €750 billion (close to 50% of GDP) of liquidity for businesses and households. In May, the government agreed on a further €55 billion (3.2% of GDP) "Relaunch" package of fiscal measures. It provided, among other things, further income support for families (€14.5 billion), funds for the healthcare system (€3.3 billion), and other measures to support businesses, including grants for SMEs and tax deferrals (€16 billion).

Spain

Key measures (about 3½% of GDP, €36 billion, subject to changes in the usage and duration of the measures) included budget support from the contingency fund to the Ministry of Health (€1.4 billion); advance transfer to the regions for the regional health services (€2.8 billion), additional funding for research related to the development of drugs and vaccines for COVID-19 (€46 million), entitlement of unemployment benefit for workers temporarily laid off under the Temporary Employment Adjustment Schemes (ERTE) due to COVID-19, with no requirement for prior minimum contribution or reduction of accumulated entitlement (€18 billion), increased sick pay for COVID-19 infected workers or those quarantined, from 60 to 75% of the regulatory base, paid by the Social Security budget (€1.4 billion).

Further, an extraordinary benefit for self-employed workers affected by economic activity suspension (€3.8 billion) was brought in. There was the introduction of a new means-tested "minimum vital income" (about €3 billion annually). This was supplemented by an unemployment protection for workers under permanent discontinuous contracts who cannot resume work but are not qualified for unemployment benefits (€99 million). Several other measures were introduced on the unemployment side to provide support to workers.

What the Indian Government could have Done?

Under these rather pressing circumstances, the government could have taken a more aggressive route on spending and tax cuts to alleviate the situation. While the additional expenditure on relief was noteworthy it affected only one section of the population and the amounts were commendable. However, at the broader level looking after displaced labour, supply chains, and unemployed were out of the periphery. So were individual taxpayers who were working on a lower salary which had to be invoked by the employers due to a halt in business. The measures taken by the government was more in terms of deferring the dates for paying tax or revoking TDS. But at the end of the day the tax had to be paid and hence came only as an operational relief and not a tax benefit. Quite clearly, all steps taken were keeping in mind the state of the fiscal deficit which as explained earlier was in jeopardy even without any affirmative action as GDP was going to fall affecting revenue collections on the tax side.

The table below gives the projections made by the IMF on the fiscal deficits of various countries for 2020. However, it does not capture the impact of loss of tax revenue which affects all countries' collections due to fall in GDP.

IMF projections of fiscal balances in Fiscal Monitor of October 2020

	2019	2020	2021
World	–3.9	–12.7	–11.8
United States	–6.3	–18.7	–17.5
Euro Area	–0.6	–10.1	–8.4
France	–3.0	–10.8	–10.6
Germany	1.5	–8.2	–5.1
Italy	–1.6	–13.0	–10.9
Spain	–2.8	–14.1	–11.7

	2019	2020	2021
Japan	–3.3	–14.2	–13.8
United Kingdom	–2.2	–16.5	–14.5
Canada	–0.3	–19.9	-20.0
Emerging Market and Middle-Income Economies	**–4.9**	**–10.7**	**–10.3**
China	–6.3	–11.9	–11.8
India	–8.2	–13.1	–11.5
Russia	1.9	–5.3	–4.6
Brazil	–6.0	–16.8	–14.5
Mexico	–2.3	–5.8	-5.2
Saudi Arabia	–4.5	–10.6	–11.7
South Africa	–6.3	–14.0	–14.2

Source: IMF

It can be assumed that the government has kept the fiscal compulsions at the forefront and treated this year as an aberration which would self-correct as the unlock process was completed and a vaccine was administered to the population. The revised deficit number for the Central Government revealed was 9.5% which means that the combined deficit of the Centre and States would be in the region of 13.5-14% as states were allowed to go to 4% with some getting the benefit of going beyond too. This was the route taken which combined relief for the poor along with a series of reforms that would work its way over the next couple of years. Maybe in a way this can be justified as the economy did show some signs of turning around post October which was a sign that probably nothing more needs to be done. The way the government presented the stimulus was that everything taken together accounted for 15% of GDP which was comparable to that of other countries. But the qualification was that a large part of it was not through the budget but through monetary support and unconditional guarantees. The 13% reflects only the slippages on revenue and meeting some of the major expenditure targets.

Chapter 17
The RBI Response

The more guidance a central bank can provide the public about how policy is likely to evolve the greater the chance that market participants will make appropriate inferences.

—Ben Bernanke

(a) The Liquidity Deluge

The announcement of the shutdown was soon followed by the RBI stepping in as the central bank to reassure the masses that it would do everything that was possible to ensure that the economy would state afloat. These words resembled those of other central banks and remained the theme till December. This was very reassuring as the Monetary Policy Committee (MPC) went in for a behind the doors meeting and made two policy announcements without public knowledge of formal meetings which took place. The decision each time was unequivocal—the economy had to be revived and for this several steps were taken. The conventional route of inflation targeting was not on the agenda and it would be "growth, growth and growth" for all purposes as there was uncertainty on the tenure of the lockdown. This was a major deviation from the assigned mandate to the MPC.

There were two policy announcements on March 27th and May 22nd. Curiously, on April 20th, the communication was that the next policy meeting would be between June 3-5, but the exigency of the shutdown and its effects compelled the MPC to meet earlier.

Let us see what the RBI said on 27th March. The MPC voted with a 4-2 majority to reduce the policy rate by 75 basis points to 4.4%. Simultaneously, the fixed rate reverse repo rate, which sets the floor of the liquidity adjustment facility (LAF) corridor, was reduced by 90 basis points to 4.0%, thus creating an asymmetrical corridor. The purpose of this measure relating to reverse repo rate is to make it relatively unattractive for banks to passively deposit funds with the Reserve Bank and instead, to use these funds for on-lending to productive sectors of the economy.

A multi-pronged approach, comprising both targeted and system-wide liquidity provision was adopted to ensure that COVID-19-related liquidity constraints are eased. The concept of Targeted Long-Term Repo Operations (TLTRO) came in. To mitigate the adverse effects on economic activity leading to pressures on cash flows across sectors, the RBI was to conduct auctions of targeted term repos of up to three years tenor of appropriate sizes for a total amount of up to ₹ 1,00,000 crore at a floating rate, linked to the policy repo rate. Liquidity availed under the scheme by banks has to be deployed in investment grade corporate bonds, commercial paper and non-convertible debentures over and above the outstanding level of their investments in these bonds as on March 25, 2020. Exposures under this facility were not to be reckoned under the large exposure framework.

Second the cash reserve ratio was lowered for banks by 100 basis points to 3.0% of net demand and time liabilities (NDTL) with effect from the reporting fortnight beginning March 28, 2020 for a period of one year. This reduction in the CRR would release primary liquidity of about ₹ 1,37,000 crore uniformly across the banking system in proportion to liabilities of constituents rather than in relation to holdings of excess SLR. This would go on to be a standard factor that would be a part of the economic stimulus package which was built by the government periodically.

The marginal standing facility (MSF) was increased from 2% of the statutory liquidity ratio (SLR) to 3% to June 30, 2020. This measure was to provide comfort to the banking system by allowing it to avail an additional ₹ 1,37,000 crore of liquidity under the LAF window in times of stress at the reduced MSF rate announced in the MPC's resolution.

These three measures relating to TLTRO, CRR, and MSF were to inject a total liquidity of ₹ 3.74 lakh crore to the system. To counter the present of persistent excess liquidity, it was decided to widen the existing policy rate corridor from 50 bps to 65 bps. Under the new corridor, the reverse repo rate under the liquidity adjustment facility (LAF) would be 40 bps lower than the policy repo rate, as against existing 25 bps. The marginal standing facility (MSF) rate would continue to be 25 bps above the policy repo rate. Quite clearly, the focus was on lowering cost and increasing availability of liquidity and inducing banks to lend to the commercial sector and not invest in government paper in the overnight market.

On 17th April, the Governor made another statement well before the policy where liquidity changes were announced. It was decided to conduct targeted long-term repo operations (TLTRO 2.0) for an aggregate amount of ₹ 50,000 crore, to begin with, in tranches of appropriate sizes. The funds availed by banks under TLTRO 2.0 was to be invested in investment grade bonds, commercial paper, and non-convertible debentures of NBFCs, with at least 50% of the total amount availed going to small and mid-sized NBFCs and MFIs. Further it was decided to provide special refinance facilities for a total amount of ₹ 50,000 crore to NABARD, SIDBI and NHB to enable them to meet sectoral credit needs. The distribution was ₹ 25,000 crore to NABARD for refinancing regional rural banks (RRBs), cooperative banks and micro finance institutions (MFIs); ₹ 15,000 crore to SIDBI for on-lending/refinancing; and ₹ 10,000 crore to NHB for supporting housing finance companies (HFCs). Advances under this facility will be charged at the RBI's policy repo rate at the time of availment.

Further, to encourage banks to deploy surplus funds in investments and loans in productive sectors of the economy, the fixed rate reverse repo rate under the liquidity adjustment facility (LAF) was lowered by 25 basis points from 4.0% to 3.75%.

On May 22nd, the MPC voted with a 5-1 majority to reduce the policy rate by 40 basis points from 4.4% to 4.0%. Consequently, the Marginal Standing Facility (MSF) rate and the bank rate stand reduced to 4.25% from 4.65%. The reverse repo rate was reduced to 3.35% from 3.75%. To enable EXIM bank to meet its foreign currency resource requirements, it was decided to extend a line of credit of ₹ 15,000 crore to the EXIM bank for a period of 90 days (with rollover up to one year) so as to enable it to avail a US dollar swap facility.

These are illustrative of the measures invoked by the RBI to enhance liquidity in the system and keep cost of borrowing low so that business could borrow and grow. Let us see the consequences of all these measures.

As stated by the government when the ₹ 20 lakh crore package was announced, the RBI's role of infusion of liquidity outside this package which got included in the package was ₹ 8 lakh crore. This came with large cuts in the repo rate which benefited all the LTRO versions which gave banks relatively permanent liquidity for period of one-three years. However, until end June or so, surplus liquidity with the banks which went into the reverse repo auctions notwithstanding the low returns of 3.35% was above ₹ 6 lakh crore on a daily basis. How can all this be explained?

The table below gives the outstanding liquidity situation since March end.

	o/n Reverse repo (daily)	LTRO o/s	TLTRO o/s	Net liquidity o/s*
24 March	3.54	1.25	Nil	–2.59
31 March	3.82	1.25	0.25	–2.53
30 April	7.48	1.25	1.13	–5.03
29 May	6.43	1.25	1.13	–3.75
30 June	6.33	1.25	1.13	–3.61
31 July	6.55	1.25	1.13	–3.83
31 Aug	6.86	1.25	1.13	–4.11
30 Sept	4.86	.01	1.13	–3.33
29 October	6.02	0.01	1.13	–4.51
29 November	6.46	0.01	1.13	–5.37
31 December	7.37	0.01	0.76	–6.25

Source: RBI

*: Repo plus MSF minus Reverse repo

The numbers cannot be added as reverse repo is for overnight deal while the others are outstanding. The purpose is to highlight the amount of surplus funds put in reverse repo auction on daily basis and the outstanding liquidity situation where negative is surplus.

From the point of view of the RBI, the picture was just about perfect with the liquidity being provided in a bundled manner for specific purposes so that there was targeting of funds. In fact, it was expected that just like there were windows opened for the NBFCs and mutual funds (₹ 50,000 crore), there could be other such facilities provided for the auto sector, real estate, hospitality, etc. But this did not happen however for some time and it was only in the December policy that the on-tap TLTROs introduced were extended to cover an additional 26 sectors besides the five sectors initially covered.

Now banks have been risk-averse and this surfeit of liquidity was not be squandered by reckless lending. Therefore, banks have been cautious with lending and have been cherry picking their clients to ensure that the quality of their asset book does not suffer. Therefore, there was a tendency to lend to the better rated clients. Hence, the surplus liquidity which came through the CRR cut and the OMOs and the earlier LTROs which were not targeted were invested primarily in the reverse repo auctions at the low rates offered by the RBI. In case of the targeted LTROs, the banks did pick up the first version for investments in bonds with alacrity but once it came to the NBFCs, they went slow as seen in the auction of ₹ 25,000 crore that elicited bids of just 50% on April 23. Quite clearly, banks did not want to go down the line.

While the job of the RBI is to provide liquidity, it cannot go ahead and force banks to lend. Therefore, as the table shows the amount going to the reverse repo auctions were very high and this was due to the willingness to lend factor. Along the way post October, the RBI had opened to window for repaying the LTROs and TLTROs. Here the response was for banks to repay them due to the existence of surplus funds. Therefore, banks no longer wanted to take on funds provided by the RBI as they were already comfortable with the deposits-credit matrix.

Bankers have been cautious because the prevailing NPA problem has hit them hard as post AQR (asset quality recognition) and the revelation of the true NPA numbers, several heads of banks have come under suspicion. Naturally, nobody wants to take a chance in lending to appease the system and run the threat of being hounded by the 3Cs in futures (CBI, CVC, CAG). Therefore, there has been hesitance shown when lending.

Even in the bond market it was noticed that while the issuance of debt paper increased post these measures, it was only the AAA and AA rated companies which were in a position to borrow. Also, these companies tended to be in the public sector and hence there was not too much enthusiasm shown for lower rated paper. Therefore, it was again a display of risk averseness in this market which is already known to be one for higher rated companies only. The TLTRO only provided a thrust to invest in the better rated companies.

Also, from the point of view of bankers they were in a fairly anomalous situation. On one hand there was a moratorium extended to all borrowers of term loans which got renewed in the May policy. Several borrowers took advantage of this move as it served them well. Now a banker who observes that a borrower has opted for the moratorium is less comfortable in extending further credit to the same party as there is apprehension built. This was another reason or banks to exercise caution while lending as moratorium have to end at some point of time after which there could be challenges.

From the borrower's perspective borrowing is not always the solution. This is so because if production has come to an end due to the shutdown which was the case, there was no point in borrowing more and building up debt unnecessarily. While the working capital limits were increased by 10% there was relief in terms of allowing companies to manage their business commitments. But borrowing for growth was ruled out as that was dependent on how the conditions would evolve.

It is not surprising that the growth in credit till June remained negative over March indicating less appetite for borrowers. As a corollary it can be said that unless the lockdown ends, and companies are able to grow only then would credit grow at a stable pace. Otherwise, it makes sense to invest in government paper which is what was observed. In fact, with the government announcing a higher borrowing programme of over ₹ 4.2 lakh crore, there was plenty of scope of this surplus liquidity to be invested in safe government paper. Add to this the State Governments which would also be going beyond the 3% fiscal deficit mark as all have been allowed to go to 3.5%, the liquidity enhancing measures could very well match the borrowing targets of the two sets of governments. In a way it could turn out to be financing by the RBI!

The table gives the incremental credit growth between March end the concerned point of time with the comparable numbers of last year to give an idea of how the system reacted to the liquidity infusion.

Incremental credit growth over March	2019	2020
End-April	–1.50	–1.01
End- May	–1.50	–1.48
End-June	-1.22	–1.25
End-July	-0.42	–1.09
End-August	-0.91	–1.59
End-September	-0.03	–0.99
End-October	0.69	–0.32
End-November	0.89	0.64
End-December	1.76	1.79

Source: RBI

The increase in credit over March, which is the base over which banks have been lending has been negative till October. This is a reflection of both willingness to lend as well as demand since during this period there have been restructuring of SME loans, moratorium to all borrowers, the credit guarantee scheme for SMEs among others which have driven this matrix.

What can be the impact of such large doses of liquidity the system? At the end of the day money is being printed by the RBI to support the economy. Most of it is likely to go into government paper and as this expenditure is more in the nature of relief, which is of revenue variety, the flow to capex is limited. In October, it was announced that there would be an additional capex of ₹ 25,000 crore which was in the nature of a stimulus.

While this is necessary, there would be a point when the excess liquidity can lead to demand pull inflation as it did post the Lehman crisis when the monetary and fiscal stimulus both kicked in simultaneously. The government would be the biggest beneficiary as it has borrowed more in the market and sustained a deficit of over 11-12% (Centre and States combined) without much strain on the system. This has obviated the debate on whether the government should be borrowing directly from the RBI which is not allowed by statute. But the route used or rather the unintended consequences of pushing liquidity in the system when there is less appetite due to a variety of reasons means that the collateral benefits have gone to the government.

(b) Bank Moratorium

When the RBI made the announcement in March on measures to support the government and the economy an interesting measure was the extending of a moratorium to the borrowers. Therefore, the statement said: Alongside liquidity measures, it is important that steps are taken to mitigate the burden of debt servicing brought about by disruptions on account of COVID-19 pandemic. Such steps, in turn, will go a long way to prevent the transmission of financial stress to the real economy, and ensure the continuity of viable businesses and provide relief to borrowers in these extraordinarily troubled times. These measures include moratorium on term loans, deferring interest payments on working capital, easing of working capital financing, deferment of implementation of the net stable funding ratio, and the last tranche of the capital conservation buffer.

In terms of actual action to be taken the RBI announced that

1. All commercial banks (including regional rural banks, small finance banks and local area banks), co-operative banks, all-India Financial Institutions, and NBFCs (including housing finance companies and micro-finance

institutions) ("lending institutions") are being permitted to allow a moratorium of three months on payment of instalments in respect of all term loans outstanding as on March 1, 2020.

2. In respect of working capital facilities sanctioned in the form of cash credit/overdraft, lending institutions are being permitted to allow a deferment of three months on payment of interest in respect of all such facilities outstanding as on March 1, 2020. The accumulated interest for the period will be paid after the expiry of the deferment period.

The moratorium on term loans and the deferring of interest payments on working capital would not result in asset classification downgrade. This is important because if not done, the banks would have had to recognize the status and accordingly make a provision which in turn would affect their profits.

Further, in respect of working capital facilities sanctioned in the form of cash credit/overdraft, lending institutions were allowed to recalculate drawing power by reducing margins and/or by reassessing the working capital cycle for the borrowers. Such changes would not result in asset classification downgrade.

The moratorium on term loans, the deferring of interest payments on working capital and the easing of working capital financing would not qualify as a default for the purposes of supervisory reporting and reporting to credit information companies (CICs) by the lending institutions. Hence, there would be no adverse impact on the credit history of the beneficiaries. In the next policy, there was an extension provided for the same.

Now the fundamental issue is that while a moratorium was something very much required as borrowers were pressurized due to the lockdown where there was no economic activity, the tendency to resort to the same was tempting. Even companies which had liquidity preferred to take the benefit as there was uncertainty regarding the state of lockdown. As there was no indication given by the government that the lockdown would end after three weeks in what became the first phase companies played safe even if they were on relatively firm ground.

The units especially in the SME sector were buffeted the most and were in need of such relief due to their business coming to an end. Also, the retail loan packet became less stable as several borrowers which were households came in the category of individuals who faced either a job loss or a harsh cut in salary. It may be recollected that the big push given by the government to housing with emphasis on affordable housing made it easier to own a home. RERA was a benefit from the point of view of the buyer. Banks too went overboard with mortgages as did the housing finance companies and other NBFCs which considered such lending to be the safest. This was because there was very good collateral available with margins being maintained in adequate quantity. Also, it is always assumed that non-performance can never happen in a wholesale manner as defaults are individual based and not as a group.

The shutdown has impacted all these three segments quite sharply. The less strong corporates especially in the services sector are most vulnerable with little certainty on their future. Second, the SMEs have been affected due to labour migration, break in supply chains and high dependence on the linked companies for survival. Third, individual borrowers would be hard pressed to repay loans if the salary income is impacted. Therefore, the moot point for every bank is to see as to how many borrowers have made use of this facility.

The table below gives an overview of the extent to which borrowers made use of the moratorium as of April 30th. As can be seen almost 50% of the customers opted for the scheme. With the exception of corporates, the moratorium was used almost evenly by all other segments. The message really is that on account of the closing of business, there was a rush for this facility as even those borrowers who had resources to fund the servicing were unsure of the future and hence preferred to use this facility. In case of individuals, it was a clear case of losing a job or taking a salary cut which made them seek solace in the moratorium as the EMIs were not affordable. In case of SMEs business halting also meant that the pile of debtors increased and so did the cash flows. This is the major takeaway from the scheme where we get an idea of the extent to which people were affected by the lockdown.

% of customers who opted for moratorium

	Corporate	MSME	Individual	Others	Total
PSBs	29	74	80	49	67
PVBs	22	21	42	39	49
FBs	33	73	8	76	21
SFBs	79	91	91	65	85
UCBs	63	67	57	36	57
NBFC	40	61	33	37	29
SCBs	25	43	52	46	55
System	**31**	**46**	**50**	**46**	**49**

% of o/s credit under moratorium

	Corporate	MSME	Individual	Others	Total
PSBs	58	82	80	64	68
PVBs	20	43	34	41	31
FBs	8	50	21	5	12
SFBs	44	52	73	12	63
UCBs	69	66	62	59	65
NBFC	56	61	46	41	49
SCBs	39	65	56	56	50
System	**42**	**65**	**55**	**55**	**50**

Source: RBI

In terms of volume of credit that was affected the table above shows again that roughly 50% of outstanding credit came under the moratorium.

The broader issue for the banking system as a whole is as to how these loans fare over time. As long as there are moratoriums the transaction is alive and is treated as a standard asset. But at some time, it would be expedient for the borrower to service the loan and repay the debt. This is where the RBI would be concerned. For the sake of transparency this data had to be shared with the public so that everyone was aware of how large this quantum could be. It was more impressionistic in nature where most bankers were saying that this was not substantial. At times it was stated that it was 10-20% of the borrowers who have opted for it. It would be in order for this to be known as the necessary action can be taken by the central bank too when withdrawing this facility. Prima facie it appeared that the first round of moratorium would have had more claimants in April as this was the time when there was virtually no top line for corporates which would have had liquidity issues. May might have been better and so would June. Getting banks to state this quantum of loans that have opted for a moratorium should ideally have been a part of the quarterly disclosures.

Within this entire set of loans that have been provided this facility, the retail segment is a concern because banks had tended to go overboard in lending here. Now with people out of jobs or living with pay cuts, servicing the debt is a challenge. While individually the amount may not be high, cumulatively could be sizable. The same holds for SMEs which till end-June were still barely operational due to the plethora of problems that emerged post the shutdown.

The RBI has to have in place a drawback plan so that bankers also are aware of how they should be treating such loans over time. One may recollect that when we went in for the AQR process in 2016 it did create a disruption as banks had to treat restructured loans as stressed loans and the recognition criteria changed which led to the ballooning of the NPAs. The same should not come as a surprise for banks and ideally the drawback plan should give banks 12-18 months to reclassify them.

Within this plan a point of dispute is whether interest should be charged on loans that are not being serviced. This pertains to interest charged on debt-servicing in the form of interest. Hence, if ₹ 100 is borrowed and the interest to be paid is ₹ 10 which is deferred according to the rules of the moratorium, then the bank should ideally charge the 10% interest on the ₹ 10 interest and the borrower must pay ₹ 11 at the end of the year. This makes banking sense as the interest earned by the bank services the deposit cost and hence logically should be levied. The other side argument is that the deferment is due to the inability of the borrower to pay because of the most unusual circumstances and hence charging an interest-on-interest payment taxes them more and goes against the ethos of the entire scheme. But given that this has to be a zero-sum game, not charging the same means a loss of income for the banking system which is already burdened with issues of quality of assets and capital.

The final decision taken is for the government to reimburse the banks on the compounding of interest. This was based on a court order and to ensure that those who paid on time are not penalized their accounts were to be credited with this amount. Hence, this step ensured that future moral hazards were not created by providing an incentive not to pay on time which is what loan waivers do at a different level. Such indirect subvention means that the money is paid out from the Budget in the form of a subsidy.

Therefore, the banking system which appeared to be getting back on its feet in FY19 and was to improve on performance in FY20 would be pushed back again by at least another year if not more depending on how these loans are treated and the accounting practices altered to finally return to normal. This is one reason as to why there is still a lot of concern on the health of the banking sector. The PSBs in particular need to be monitored closely as this is where there could be talk from above to deal with the moratorium compared with private banks. But for sure things will not be the same for them in FY21.

Status of Moratorium as of August 2020

The table below gives the status of loans under moratorium. As can be seen 38% of overall credit and 43% of customers had opted for this scheme as of August which was three months post the unlocking process.

	Corporate	MSMEs	Individuals	Others	Total
As % o/s credit	30.4	68.1	33.9	39.1	37.9
As % of total customers	18.0	77.2	43.6	35.6	43.8

Source: RBI

The interesting takeaway from this table is that in April around 50% of total customers and o/s credit was under moratorium. This has improved to 38% for credit and 44% for number of customers. These numbers nevertheless are quite high indicating a combination of distress as well as uncertainty. However, what stands out is that this proportion has increased quite sharply for MSMEs from 65% to 77% in terms of proportion of customers and 43% to 68% for o/s credit. This is notwithstanding the emergency credit line that was extended by the government for this segment. While it is possible that more MSMEs have opted for this scheme due to the relief provided and not because of inherent inability, this does raise a flag on possible future NPAs arising. For the other segments there has been a reduction in the proportion of loans and customers under moratorium. The challenge really will be for banks to prepare for the same so that the requisite provisions are made to ensure that they do not counter other barriers on the capital raising front.

(c) Emergency Line of Credit

One of the rather innovative schemes brought out by the government which was started for the SMEs and then extended to other targeted sectors was the ECLGS. The genesis of the same is interesting. The sector most affected by the lockdown was the SMEs. Given their nature, they were affected on both the demand and supply side and with payments held back by the government and other companies, were driven to a corner. Getting credit was a challenge as they were clearly not creditworthy. So what did the government do?

This emergency line of credit guarantee was invoked wherein the SMEs that were performing as of March 1, 2020 could get credit up to 20% of their outstanding credit as of that date with an interest rate ceiling of 9.5% with a four year repayment period including one year moratorium. This was provided till October, which was extended to November and finally to March 2021. The upper ceiling was ₹ 3 lakh crore of sanctions. Now with total outstanding credit to the SMEs in the region of ₹ 11 lakh crore, if every unit qualified the maximum could have been ₹ 2.2 lakh crore of disbursements given the ratio of 75% for outstanding as proportion of sanctions.

The SMEs felt that the clause of units being performing at the time of March 2020 was not justified as these units would have anyway had access to credit and it was the ones which were distressed that required such support. The scheme was extended further to sole proprietorships and other businessmen so that they could use this facility. Hence, the perimeter that was defined to qualify for such loans was restrictive. The government had argued that in the Atmanirbhar package there were separate dispensations for those under stress as well as those that were doing well (the equity contribution scheme discussed earlier).

The success of this scheme was advertised on social media and it was surprising that there was no official press release as such. Ideally, a formal approach would have been expected from the government though the FM did state in the AN-3 package the sanctioned amount here.

Guarantees under ECLGS (₹ lakh crore)

2020	Sanctioned	Disbursed	Ratio of D/S
June 18	0.40	0.21	52.5
July 4	1.14	0.66	57.8
September 7	1.61	1.13	70.2
October 5	1.87	1.37	73.3
November 2	2.03	1.48	72.9
December 5	2.05	1.59	77.5

Source: Media Reports

There were some interesting views expressed by the SME segment. First as mentioned earlier, it was meant for those units which were performing. Hence, it did not include those under stress. The government had provided for some element of restructuring for them but new credit was not part of the deal. Second, for a SME to access funds there had to be a purpose. When demand was down for their products or they were not functional due to the absence of labour or inputs there was less need for fresh capital for investment or even working capital purposes. Third, keeping a limit of 20% was considered by some as being on the lower side as those that were expanding wanted this to be open ended. True, the government could not guarantee all loans. The scheme basically was a loan guarantee for all MSMEs which were performing as on February 29th with an outstanding of ₹ 25 crore (increased to ₹ 50 crore when the same was extended to November) where 20% incremental credit up to ₹ 5 crore (now ₹ 10 crore) would be covered.

The interesting thing was that data on credit to this segment revealed an interesting possibility.

Date	o/s (₹ lakh crore)	Change ₹ crore
May 22	10.78	NA
June 19	11.32	46,000
July 31	11.00	–32,000
Aug 28	11.04	4,000
Sep 25	11.27	23,000
Oct 23	11.25	–20,000

Source: RBI

While the government spoke of sanctions crossing ₹ 2 lakh crore and outstanding being around 75% of the total, the incremental credit to this sector based on RBI data was just about ₹ 50,000 crore by September-end. What does this indicate? It shows that money borrowed was used for repayments and was not used for either fresh working capital or investment. This is important because the scheme gave these performing units a chance to repay their loans by taking fresh credit, which came at a lower price as the cost was capped at 9.25% which was of advantage to the borrowers and a cost for the bank. The loan being guaranteed by the government provided solace to the banks even though there was a lower income to be earned by banks.

Any which way this scheme can be interpreted as a relief for the borrowers even if it was just used for repaying old loans. The AN-3 package which came towards the festival time extended this scheme now for non-SME companies too with exposures of between ₹ 50-500 crore. This again would help units repay old loans in the 26 identified stressed sectors as per the Kamath Committee.

The question often asked is that if the entire result tended to be companies using this facility for repaying loans, the scheme could be more all-encompassing for companies. This way the benefit would be to all sectors. The implication for banks would be different.

While they would have the comfort of government guarantee for these loans, in case they were used to repay old loans, then the cost would be borne by the banks. In fact as these loans would be repaid over four years including a moratorium, the cost would be fixed for this time period. Typically, SMEs get funds at above 12% while the others could be getting at closer to the benchmark rate which can be the TBill or GSec chosen by the bank. There is hence a loss of income for the bank which can be anywhere between 200-300 bps. The banks will call it a loss of income as the rate has been fixed by the government and there is no subsidy being provided for them. The fact that these are standard assets of SMA-0 (Special Mention Accounts) loans means that there was a low probability of default and would have been serviced at a higher rate as per the original terms of engagement. It should be remembered that any scheme involving banks which has interest rates being fixed is a zero sum game. In case borrowers gain on lower interest rates, evidently the bank is earning less. Hence if ₹ 1 lakh crore of the ECLGS scheme was used for repayment, the lower interest received for every 1% interest rate compromise by banks would mean ₹ 1000 crore.

Hence, it does appear that this scheme is once again one where the cost is being borne outside the government and while the guarantee is there, it is a contingent liability and does not involve any budgetary outlay as such.

(d) One-time Restructuring

The government and RBI had worked hard to alleviate the financial stress accorded to companies on account of the lockdown. The first related to the moratorium which got extended till August. This gave time to borrowers to service their debt without being called defaulters. As a reward to those who did not take the moratorium there was a reimbursement made by the government for the imputed interest on interest—a contentious subject given that the courts had ruled that those loans under moratorium cannot be charged interest on unpaid interest. SMEs got the emergency line of credit for ₹ 3 lakh crore which was guaranteed by the government as well as extension of the restructured loans. This left the non-SMEs out of the frame.

To address the servicing commitments of the large companies thee Reserve Bank had, on August 7, 2020, announced the constitution of an Expert Committee under the chairmanship of Shri K.V. Kamath to make recommendations on the required financial parameters to be factored in the resolution plans under the 'Resolution Framework for Covid19-related Stress' along with sector specific benchmark ranges for such parameters.

The committee recommendations were not to be applicable for personal loans and the SME borrowers. The framework enabled lending institutions including NBFCs, which are an essential part of the lenders' pool under this Framework, to implement a Resolution Plan (RP) in respect of eligible corporate exposure even without change in ownership while classifying such exposure as Standard, subject to specified conditions.

The main objective of the committee was to identify suitable financial parameters that should be factored into the assumptions underlying resolution plan (RP) finalized by the lending institutions under the Resolution Framework. The parameters were to cover aspects related to leverage, liquidity, debt serviceability, etc.

Further, the committee was to recommend sector-specific ranges for such financial parameters that will serve as boundary conditions for the resolution plan (RP). The committee could also make any other recommendations relating to financial or non-financial conditions to be considered for the RP, within the contours of the framework announced by the Reserve Bank of India.

The committee was to undertake the process validations of RP submitted in respect of borrowers where the aggregate exposure of the lending institutions at the time of invocation of the resolution process is ₹ 1500 crore and above. The process validation entailed verification of the RP in terms of their adherence to the conditions prescribed in the Resolution, without interfering with the commercial judgement exercised by the lenders.

Key Highlights of Resolution Framework dated August 6, 2020 were the following.

Eligibility

- Resolution under this Framework extended only to borrowers having stress on account of Covid-19.
- Only those borrowers which were classified as standard and with arrears less than 30 days as on March 1, 2020 are eligible under the Framework.

Invocation date and implementation:

- Resolution Framework may be invoked not later than December 31, 2020.
- RP needs to be implemented within 180 days from the date of invocation.

The committee identified 26 sectors for this purpose and specified the parameters and the limits within which the company would qualify for such a restructuring. There were five metrics that were considered here. These were:

- Total Outside Liability/Adjusted Tangible Net Worth (TOL/Adjusted TNW)
- Total Debt/EBIDTA
- Current Ratio
- Debt Service Coverage Ratio (DSCR)
- Average Debt Service Coverage Ratio (ADSCR)

The initial estimate made on the volume of debt that could go for restructuring was in the range of ₹ 3-5 lakh crore, the progress of the same would be known probably by the end of the year.

There can be no opposition to the one-time restructuring process but some points have to be noted. It has been observed that almost all schemes on restructuring tend to be extended for several years. This will be possible again here especially so as one can never be sure of when the problems afflicting industry will be overcome. This is important because any such exercise involved not just the tenure of the loan being extended and not being classified as a NPA, but the cost of finance, i.e. the lending rate is lowered to help the borrowers. This means that there would inherently be a loss of income for banks as all such exercises are a zero-sum game and a lower cost for the borrower is lower income for the lender. As there is no subsidy being provided by the government unlike the case of 'interest on interest under the moratorium' it is but natural that the cost has to be borne by the banks.

But this OTR can be considered to be one of the more proactive steps taken by the RBI to assist units under stress due to the covid lockdown. In a way, it can be said that the entire set of borrowers have been helped through various measures by the government and the RBI on the credit side to ensure that there are no financial pressures of debt servicing at a time when their P&L accounts have been under pressure.

Therefore, on the aspect relating to servicing of debt, the RBI has brought in several schemes to ensure that those entities which can be individuals were stressed due to the lockdown are provided space for serving debt. The moratorium was the immediate measure that gave relief to everyone. The emergency line of credit was to enhance the flow of credit to the SMEs as they were not in a position to draw enhanced credit from the system due to the risk involved. Their loans have already been under the restructuring net and the plans need to be implemented by December 2021.

Going ahead what has to watched out for is how these loans perform. The emergency line of credit, restructured advances of both SMEs and others, would all have to start performing at some point of time or else the threat of a sharp increase in NPAs cannot be ruled out. While the problem has been addressed today, it has been deferred and not resolved. This has been a constant challenge for the banking system and banks too are aware of these possible problems.

How to Look at the Overall Action taken by the Government and RBI?

First for the government. It was clear that the lockdown was imposed in a haste out of a sense of panic rather than a well thought plan. This was understandable as it was never known how the spread of infection would progress. Having gone in for a three-week lockdown with no tangible results being witnessed, it was but natural that the lockdown was extended. The problems were not foreseen, and it was never known as to which segments would be affected and to what extent. Therefore, the approach was to identify a problem like that of the migrants and then address the same with some policy responses. Again, the implementation part was open to interpretation at various levels of the government and hence the instructions from above were seldom adhered to along the way.

The immediate response of the government which came along with the lockdown was the relief measures which was commendable, though were of a short-term nature. Promising free food to people and cash transfers were laudable announcements but the delivery part was always going to be tough. Getting the NREGA programme to start functioning from the beginning of the year was easier as this system has already been firmly entrenched in the country and hence was a success. The other measures announced like deferment of provident funds payments or tax refunds were more administrative in nature.

The RBI on its part was fast to react and the measures on the liquidity front were laudable as this is what was within its purview. Cutting rates, enhance the flow of liquidity to various sections through the CRR cuts and repo transactions were quick. But the RBI has no control over demand and when units were shut the problem was how to service existing debt and not take on more of it. This is where the moratorium helped as it gave more breathing space to borrowers which was required. This worked well for all borrowers including those who had the ability to service their debt but were uncertain of the future.

One consequence of lowering the interest rates was that it affected the savers quite sharply. Bringing down repo rate was accompanied by the small savings rates being reduced by the government which served a double whammy for the fixed income class. While the salaried workers were affected by lower pay and silence over increments besides reduction in the variable pay, the retired gentry which depend on interest on deposits and other forms of savings that are linked to these administered interest rates for sustenance found themselves in a tight spot. The beneficiary was the government which had an expansive borrowing programme that was now coming cheaper both in the form of lower rates on market borrowings as well as lower outflows on interest on the NSSF (National Small Savings Fund). This has never been highlighted as a cost of the pandemic which was imposed from above. The repercussions were indirect on the government as lower income reduced the spending power of households that affected consumption and in turn the tax collections, especially GST.

The Atma Nirbhar packages which spanned seven months were better planned and not spontaneous as were the announcements made at the time of the lockdown. Here one can say that the package blew hot and cold on what was to have an impact immediately and what was to have a longer term impact. Similarly, it was unclear as to how much of the allocations spoken of were to be reckoned in the current year of crisis and how much would be futuristic. Further, by mixing the role of the RBI in providing liquidity as part of the package, the numbers tended to be overstated.

Several measures were in the nature of reforms and went with the Atma Nirbhar strategy but should not have been confused with relief for the people as the two were separate issues. The Economic Survey for 2020-21 has reaffirmed the unique approach that the government took which was not followed anywhere else in the world—a combination of relief with reforms agenda. Interestingly, the Budget for 2021-22 showed that the government had actually transferred a lower amount under the PM Kisan Scheme and while spending on employment schemes was aggressive the food relief had terminated by end of 2020 and was not provided for in the coming year.

The package was hence a new policy framework in the nature of reforms that looked at all sectors and had a longer term in mind. The fact that this was blended with measures to aid consumption did make it difficult to separate the two. Also measures like giving advances to government employees or allowing them to use their LTC to finance a consumer good which had to cost a multiple time the basic price, was not really an incentive as people were allowed to use their own money and the move did not involve any additional funding.

Even the credit measures though laudable were indirect in the sense that the borrowers had to use the funds for economic activity and was not really a giveaway. This is why when compared with what was offered by other countries in the form of tax cuts and cash transfers to all people, this particular package of ₹ 30 lakh crore was very different. Therefore, it was never called a fiscal stimulus by the government but a plain economic stimulus. Analysts however took it as a fiscal stimulus and erroneously started calculating the impact on the fiscal deficit which actually did not make any sense. Hence, while the FM did often talk about financing of this stimulus, a very limited amount was coming from the budget per se and hence the flow from institutions like PFC to DISCOMs or NABARD to the agricultural banking system did not involve outlays as such. The ₹ 3 lakh crore of guaranteed lending to SMEs was from banks and the Kisan Credit cards amount of ₹ 2 lakh crore was credit being given in the normal course of activity. The government would come into the frame on the SME loans after four years if there were defaults.

It is hence important to interpret these numbers in an appropriate manner. The common man did not get any income tax relief and while the very poor got free food, the flow stopped after the festival season even while work was still not available. Enterprises that had to close down due to restrictions are out of business with the workforce being unemployed and will have to strive hard to find alternative work. States had promised to create alternative jobs in their territory, but it is still not certain as to the progress made here. In fact, after the unlock programme was announced, it was assumed that things would gradually return to normal and hence there were no further announcements made by the states.

It could be hence said that the stimulus from the government had fiscal implications in FY21 even without any excess spending and the deficit was more due to fall in revenue. As such, slippages on revenue were sharp and hence the government was cognizant of the same and spent money in a measured manner. A counter view would be that in a year like 2020 where all countries were extravagant with aid for the people, it may not have mattered if the government had been more aggressive in its outlays to ensure that the suffering of the citizens was alleviated. But this issue can always be debated on both ends.

How about the RBI? The RBI did what could be done but with demand being limited, borrowers were able to lower their cost of debt and borrow more at the margin for survival rather than for growth. That has been the trend all through that much of the lending that has taken place is to keep enterprise afloat rather than bring about higher investment for growth. This gets translated in the expected fall in capital formation. The concern going ahead is when the entire system of restructuring ends and the true quality of assets of the banking system is known. That is something that the central bank would be keeping a close watch.

Ruminations

Chapter 18
Industries that must Reinvent

So little time
Try to understand that I'm
Trying to make a move just to stay in the game
I try to stay awake and remember my name
But Everybody's Changing, and I don't feel the same

—Keane: Everybody's changing

The virus impact through the economic shutdown has also exposed the vulnerabilities of several sectors that will see a different kind of future. The progressive growth rate that was assumed for several consumer-oriented industries will see a change in direction and pace as the new reality sets in fully. The virus impact in terms of how long it can last is unknown and the best response is that we have to all learn to live with it. This means that everyone has to adjust to the new world where certain norms have to be pursued for an undefined period of time.

Also given that the countries which thought that the worst was over have also witnessed a relapse though of much milder forms is indicative that things have not yet returned to normal. More importantly nothing is certain of the future. The signal really is that at any point of time there can be the strike-back of the virus which will further push economies back.

While a vaccine is a solution it is uncertain on how long it will take to successfully cover the population across the world and whether it is a foolproof solution. There is already some debate on whether the new strains of the virus can be countered by the existing known vaccines. Countries should ideally be better prepared for such an epidemic in future as the experimentation has been conducted in this episode with mixed results. But the response of some of the Western developed countries to the second wave appears to be a replication of what was done earlier and hence an alternative plan may not have yet been in place with a lockdown being the only solution. Hopefully, government reactions will be better.

There is clearly no single size that fits all as what worked in some countries like a lockdown has not worked in India. For example, the 21 days lockdown to begin with should have ideally ensured that all those who were infected were traced and treated. While there were erring people during this period who did not sit at home for different reasons, there was no reason to believe that by July the number would escalate past a million. But still the government and health departments now know how to impose a lockdown and how to define containment zones and keep testing people for the infection. To this extent it is valuable knowledge gained which will help to counter future attacks.

Now what are going to be the rules of engagement for sure for another couple of years for certain because it will take a very long time before India moves out of the state of not moving around in masks when out of home. This can be a certainty which cannot be contested. This will be the starting point of conjecturing the rules of the game.

Second the concept of social distancing will be a part of our culture and this becomes important as it will be affecting business in different ways. Indians as a rule tend to flock together as it is part of culture where every festival is celebrated together. Also, as a rule people don't mind touching one another and the western concept of private space never existed. The new rules will mean that these distances have to be maintained and also go into the way we go about our lives.

Third, the impact of the lockdown with compulsory closure of most offices has brought about a sea change in the way in which businesses proceeded. Where corporate offices were involved people have moved over to the concept of work-from-home which was a new concept and something most people could not ever think of doing. While some offices especially in the IT sector had this concept of working from home, they were the exceptions rather than the rules. Now the rules have been rewritten and even when normalcy—if ever there is one—is attained the working psyche has changed and the WFH concept will be part of the system.

Fourth, there will be more concern on the health front where people become more conscious of disease especially those related to viral infections. Besides individuals who get affected by these afflictions, the people around would be in a state of paranoia. The response to future possible epidemics at the micro level will be swifter as this covid pandemic has caused irreparable damage across all geographies. This will also mean that people will seek out health cover regularly to cover all eventualities.

Fifth, people in the business community have gotten in the mold of conducting meetings through the web which has been quite successful and efficient. This paradigm has to be kept in mind going forward as it will have a bearing on the way business is conducted. This was inconceivable a year back. But doing so today helps time and money for companies and could be the new normal.

Sixth, the daily chores of running households have moved significantly from physical shopping to ecommerce which will accelerate in future. The online shopping mode which caught on earlier due to novelty now is preferred for convenience. Dependency on house help will no longer taken to be given and will be susceptible to change.

These conjectures are important because these habits will cause a paradigm shift in the way in which several industries have to reorient their business. The demand drivers are going to change and, in some cases, could be of a permanent nature. Therefore, it would be necessary for industries to redevelop their strategies so that the goals are in sync with the changing environment.

Hospitality

Hospitality is one industry which would have to completely redefine the approach to business in the light of this pandemic. We have already seen that this segment of business is the lowest in the pecking order in terms of being a part of the 'unlock' programme of the government. This in turn means that it would take a longer time to recover. Hotels need to look at their models closely.

The three main drivers of revenue for hotels are room occupancy, dining and conferences. All three levers are likely to be in for a long haul towards recovery. Occupancy is normally driven by business travelers for the starred hotels and this includes both global and domestic individuals. Companies have been conducting meetings over the web which comes at a low cost. As companies work towards cutting costs, there would be a tendency to opt for web-based meetings rather than physical meetings which will make stay in hotels unnecessary. Further, business travelers would also be apprehensive of staying in hotels even after the lockdown ends for fear of getting infected. This fear psychosis may override the 'entitlement' factor which made business executives travel and stay in hotels. Admittedly, after a point of time normalcy will be restored as in the corporate world travel and stay are considered to be perquisites once a person reaches a certain position. But from the point of view of the hotels industry working with excess capacity for the next couple of years may be a reality.

Leisure travelers would now become the mainstay for the hospitality industry which had to entice them with better deals including safety. But the response of this section would vary and cannot be conjectured for sure and get linked also to how easy it is to travel across geographies both form other countries and within India and the availability of convenient modes of transport. The response of domestic travelers has been positive post the opening up of this industry and occupancy rates have improved for resorts-based structures. But international travel as of December 2021 had several restrictions and most of the passengers moving were more for returning to their homes rather than for leisure.

The second and third waves of the virus has affected travel even within the euro zone with UK being blacklisted temporarily. Such shock waves cannot be ruled out any time during the year as long as countries are not vaccinated fully.

Another second driver of business is conferences, and this is going to be a major blow for the industry. While the Indian penchant of holding conferences and business meetings in hotels has always been a status symbol, the same has been replicated even over the web of late quite seamlessly. In fact, several conferences have been able to also charge for the participation and hence may just consider holding them in this mode. This means hotels have to look at how this space would be used. Personal functions like marriages would still return to this mode over a period of time, but the industry will have to look at ways of using this space commercially to ensure that their business remains profitable. The hotels industry does serious business with the conference halls and while like business travel would return to normal over a period of time, using the space for alternative activity would be a part of business plans.

The dining segment would also have to reinvent itself to cater to the changing environment where social distancing has to be maintained which will mean lowering the capacity in the restaurants that will impact the revenue flowing. Several hotels in India were operating with minimal eating and restricted timing in their restaurants especially for non-resident guests.

Economic Times reported on the IBIS hotel group. Hotels chain Ibis said it had introduced alternative working space for individuals and organisations in India in adherence to the safety and hygiene standards amid COVID-19 crisis. Available across all its properties in India, the new Work@ibis provided a safe, alternative working space to individuals and organisations looking to work remotely in a healthy and reliable environment. The service featured ready-to-move-in workspaces, meeting and conference rooms and lounges with access to high-speed Internet connectivity, essentials, tea and coffee station, and customised F&B offerings. These spaces are stringently sanitised in adherence to the Accor group's All safe global cleanliness and prevention standards and Indian Government norms. This is an example of adaptation made by a particular hotel chain which would be a part of business plans for others too.

Automobiles

This is another segment which will witness cross currents which can affect the final outcome. Let us see what works in the favour of the industry. With social distancing being the norm, there would-be reluctance to travel by public transport and the natural corollary would be higher demand for automobiles and depending on the income level of the person the choice would be between a two-wheeler and a car. This will increase demand for vehicles in general also leading to more congestion on the roads. In particular, two wheelers would be preferred by people in larger cities on account of adapting to congestion.

A countervailing force would be in the form of lower demand due to greater propensity to work from home and offices also preferring to have their staff operate from home to save on office space. This will lower the demand for vehicles which would be used more for leisure activity rather than for commuting to place of work. Several offices have given up space and introduced the norm of partial working from home where staff come to office on rotation and make do with the existing or truncated office space. This makes travel less of a concern and hence the need to own a vehicle may come down.

As long as these new trends emerge and get cemented, the industry will have to keep this factor in mind.

Real Estate

This industry too will have to contend with differing forces. With companies now realizing that staff can operate from home quite efficiently there can be a reduction in demand for office space. Hence, commercial property will definitely see a decline and this sector has to be prepared for the same. We have also seen an increase in co-working spaces in urban India where professionals have preferred to rent out pace in common offices where overheads get defrayed over the tenants. Over the months of lockdown where everyone operated from home the tenants have realized that it is also possible to do business from home and hence would reconsider their options. Therefore, this entire business concept would be in jeopardy and the spaces that have been set up over the last few years would function with lower capacity utilization. This can lead to fall in rents and hence income for the promoters.

Commercial property also is manifested in malls and retail set ups. The impact of covid has had a sharp impact on both of them. Companies with their own showrooms had perforce to close in the first couple of months of the lockdown and would reconsider options based on the demand. This holds for garments, toys, cosmetics, phones, electronics, etc. Competition from the ecommerce format always existed and will increase sharply under these conditions. Malls had already reached the stage of having surplus capacity in big cities and will be challenged further with entry restrictions and SOPs affecting footfalls. Therefore, construction of new structures will witness a slowdown.

Even on the residential front there would be developments that can change the way in which people live and hence affect the realty players. Metropolitan cities and other urban areas which have been afflicted with the pandemic may not be the first choice for most people looking to buy houses. Congestion and slums would be influencing factors and while people may be forced to work where jobs exist, where choices exist would be exercised. Similarly, the penchant for having multiple homes in places like Mumbai and Delhi would be a thing of the past as investments in satellite towns and cities would make more sense in terms of cleaner living.

One may hope that the long-lasting impact of the pandemic would be change in living where hygiene dominates and people in cities also modify their way of living. This can mean creation of more homes that are spread out in the distant suburbs which offers benefits of social distancing and rather than live in crowded tenements which is the case in industrial-based-slums people prefer to live outside the city and commute to be safe. Individuals also would have to look for more space at home as families closeted in small apartments cannot manage business, education, and leisure in the limited space as family members fight for space and network connection.

These are possibilities and while one can never be sure of how individuals react, the commercial part of the story will definitely rule and hence real estate developers will have to be prepared for such a changing scenario.

Entertainment

Going to a concert or a movie was always a family outing and hence a social occasion. Theatres offer little scope for social distancing in the normal course as people meet and mingle in the waiting area before moving into the theatre and then watching the show. Covid has impacted this entire experience in more than many ways.

This business is lower down the pecking order and survives on ticket sales, which get linked to advertisements and finally food and beverage sales. The future course of opening up of this business is fuzzy. To begin with the SOPs would be in place where fewer can watch the show and would have to enter the theatre directly without waiting outside. Managing F&B will have their own challenges and the fear of consumption to begin with will make demand scarce. The experience will no longer be there, and this is one reason as to why kickstarting the business will be difficult.

Also, in terms of demand for entertainment, the lockdown has brought about a change in which people fulfill this goal. Watching movies at home and the live streaming that is available has substituted the experience to an extent and people may find it hard to make a change given the variety and contemporary nature of the watch from home option.

These changing trends will affect the production houses and distribution channels which will perforce reinvent their models. This will have far-reaching effects on the industry as all production of entertainment get linked with the advertising world involving sponsorships and other backward linkages with the chains involved. It will be a modified version of creative destruction as new approaches to entertainment will challenge the existing structures. The latter have to work hard on ensuring that their business models survive. Theatres for example will have to keep in mind the fact that there would be fewer films released through this mode and viewership different. There was already sown the seeds of change by the Netflix and Amazon Prime channels which were catering to niche segments to begin with before the pandemic. Things could change now with the masses being exposed to home entertainment. Such a disruption will be serious for this segment.

Aviation

The airline sector has wide ranging linkages with not just companies involved in transporting people but also aircraft's builders, service providers, etc. *The Economist* had reported some interesting data on the airlines industry and related sectors which can give an idea of how important this sector is.

It was estimated that in 2019 around 4-5 billion passengers travelled in the skies. On an average there could have been around 100,000 commercial flights every day. According to the Air Transport Action Group around 10 million jobs could have been involved in these operations. These would be about six million at airports, including staff of shops and cafés, luggage handlers, cooks of in-flight meals and the like, another 2.7 million airline workers and 1.2 million employees in manufacturing aircraft. The revenue earned on the whole was around $170 billion for the airports and around $838 billion for the airlines.

The two major manufacturers of planes, Airbus and Boeing had sales of $100 billion between them. For the aerospace industry as a whole they were perhaps $600 billion. Travel firms when added would have resulted in annual revenues of some $1.3 trillion in normal times for listed firms alone.

This is one segment that has to reinvent itself for sure in India. The airlines industry has always been under stress of high debt and high losses. Some have managed to break this link at times, but more often than not succumbed to this syndrome. The shutdown impact on this industry has been sharp and will continue to be challenging.

Travelers are of two types, business, and leisure. Both the engines need to fire to keep the industry going and there are problems here. Business travelers will take time to come back as the work from home practice has shown that business can be conducted from home and one need not travel to places to meet clients, customers or officials. This new style of working has benefited companies too which have saved on cost as the work is being conducted through technology without moving out. While traveling to other places has conventionally been considered to be an entitlement or perquisite especially as one moved up the corporate echelon, companies would be more discerning from now on. Also, executives may be apprehensive of travel and hence may prefer to do from home. Besides the fear syndrome there would also be the willingness of companies to pay for such travel which in turn will be linked to overall business prospects. In the interim period airlines will have to figure out how to stay profitable as it could take at least two years for normalcy to come in when the vaccine hopefully addresses the fear factor and a turnaround in corporate fortunes enables travel.

The leisure travelers have already shown some positive signs by being willing to travel notwithstanding the fear of the virus. But for normalcy to be restored it would be essential for the vaccination cycle to be completed so that there is less doubt. Until such time the possibility of state-level restrictions on travel can be expected. As late as December the world including India had put an embargo on international flights while passengers from different states had special checks for entering others. Such idiosyncratic behaviour cannot be escaped and can affect flow of traffic. Therefore, airlines have to adjust their pricing and costs keeping in mind that the capacity utilization levels would be fairly volatile.

Retailing through Brick and Mortar

The lockdown made everyone turn to ecommerce and supermarket options where available. Certain large players have managed to capture the wallet share of customers during this time period and made major forays of investment in this area by delivering groceries at competitive prices. E-commerce always had the advantage of convenience where doorstep delivery made it an attractive option. Amazon in particular has made substantial gains in this area of 'pantry business' which had scaled up substantially over this period. This is not good news for the local retail store of the mom-and-pop variety. Their business was affected to begin with by irregular and erratic supplies which made it difficult to address the demand of customers. This was the time when Amazon, Flipkart and the other existing platforms like Big Basket and Grofers were able to leverage their financial clout and supply chains to enter the doors of several households. The local *kiranas* will find it hard to make up for this lost ground and given the limited financial wherewithal would probably have to wind up at some point of time. Such business in rural areas will still survive but metro and larger urban areas would see a distinct transition.

Education

The transformation witnessed in the education sector has been quite remarkable as the lockdown continues to this sector even till January. Assuming that to some extent there will be opening up of schools and colleges across the country in the coming year one may expect normalcy to return at some point of time. Education is a sector which has constant growing demand whether it is institutional which involves providing certificates and degrees as well as support services like coaching. Students will always return to the classroom as it is believed that development of children requires a certain degree of social interaction. This cannot be avoided. And as most institutions which are providing primary, secondary, college, professional courses are finally linked with government-run Boards or universities there will never be the case of close down.

The interesting conjecture is however on how education is conducted. Textbooks may be a thing if the past as all books are digitized and provided online to students. The question is that the publishing industry which relies a lot on education has to rethink the models. Coaching classes which so far have been working on a model of physical attendance can do the same job through online classes with passwords to ensure that there is screening of attendance. This saves a lot of time for students in traveling as well as cost for the owners of the institutes which has a bearing on commercial rents and hence the real estate sector. A shift to the distance mode appears to be a win-win situation for all concerned.

Several schools especially at the higher end of fees may just prefer to keep classes online as it is an efficient solution. Students do not have to come to class which saves time and enables parents to send their children to coaching classes which unfortunately has become a habit these days. But such an action will affect ancillary services that are linked to schools such as the transport network that gets linked to children going to school.

How about manufacturing? Prima facie it appears that there may be less disruption in future going by the way things have evolved post lockdown. For example, it was noticed that industries like vegetable oils and beverages like coffee and tea had witnessed lower demand with the bulk segments comprising airports, hotels, restaurants, offices remaining closed for the first couple of months. However, with the gradual opening up of these segments, demand has started to return. But for sure change in office environment with fewer people visiting the premises will lower demand for beverages and hence even the food segment which thrived on the office demand will witness a change. The same holds for airports where declining demand due to fewer passengers will question the viability of all the outlets in the food as well as fine living products usually on display here. In fact, with international travel down to levels of 40-50% of normal due to country restrictions survival of shops and restaurants in airports would be in jeopardy thus affecting jobs as well as the profitability of the establishments.

Hence, while manufacturing per se is better placed compared with services, the secondary impact cannot be ruled out at the margin. The fall in demand for new malls or office space affects not just the real estate sector but also the industries in the backward chain like cement, steel, cables, etc. Manufacturing too will be in for some shake-up in the coming years though the extent may be hard to conjecture presently.

Chapter 19
Epilogue

A government is the most dangerous threat to man's rights: it holds a legal monopoly on the use of physical force against legally disarmed victims.

—Ayn Rand

The economic lockdown in India was the first of its kind and in retrospect does appear to have been quite meaningless. While defenders of the move would argue that it had to be done as all countries were doing it and that the spread of infection would have been more monstrous, critics would aver that it did not help to stop the infection from spreading and hence was a mis-step. In fact, under the force of circumstances the government did unlock the economy from June onwards even as the infection levels spread substantially. The lockdown consequences were grim as seen in various economic aspects where there was suffering.

The lockdown and its progress exposed the absence of coordination between the Centre and States and it is probably for the first time in post-independence history that a singular measure was taken at the national level, but States ran their rules depending on their perception. For the first time States blanked out movement of persons and goods from other states more out of fear than anything else. Therefore, even till as late as December, there was strong sense of disorientation. The government was hence still in a state of not exactly knowing how to go about the job of restoring normalcy. The solution for rising incidence of infections in any state was to have some kind of a lockdown to stop activity. As of February 2021 Karnataka put restrictions on people coming from Kerala as there was a surge in the number of infected people in this state.

The curious development was that once the talk of the vaccine dominated the headlines attention got diverted from the unlock strategy which came to an end. Therefore, opening up of suburban trains, permitting higher attendance in offices, recommencing education institutions, etc. was left to individual States and the Centre stopped talking of this road of normalcy. It looked like that the Centre would speak about the vaccination programme and for all practical purposes there was going to be no talk on the roadmap for further unlocking. Even within States there was no thought given to the localized restrictions as it was assumed that the status quo would prevail. In January, India had reached a stable position in terms of covid cases which was in the bracket of 15000-20000. Maharashtra had put mandatory testing on people arriving from Delhi, Rajasthan, Gujarat and Goa in November as the incidence was high in these States. But in January when these States ceased to be stressed, the restrictions were not lifted. The cost and inconvenience caused was immense but as usual in India, who cares?

This again was not really unusual as even in Europe when the second wave unleashed countries the response was to have lockdowns. However, there were lessons learnt from the first episode and the new lockdowns were diluted. But for sure, social life was put behind the door and therefore the Indian response was also not out of the ordinary.

The public at large was inconvenienced a lot during the lockdown, but did not protest at all against government action. In a way it was quite a stoical way of going through hardship. This is quite a contrast to the protest of farmers in the north to the Farm Laws that were passed—where the fear was based on hypothetical situations evolving in future. The State Elections of Bihar showed that the voters do not mind any discomfort as a large part of the migrant population was from this State. People were on the roads for weeks together with helpless state governments trying to get them home. The government at the Centre and the coalition at the State should have been ideally targeted by the voters. But this was not to be. This goes to show that either there was acceptance of the actions of the government or *karma*. The same coalition came back to power quite convincingly. In fact, while it was widely expected by the intelligentsia that the voters would be angry over demonetization of 2016 in the Elections of 2019, it did not matter. Either memory was too short, or the voters were convinced that demonetization did a lot of good by getting rid of black money. Or even more likely people just forget the incident. Electorates in India are more sensitive to moral misdemeanor than adverse economic policies. Interestingly, in the USA Presidential Elections one of the contributing factors for the loss of Elections was the inability of Donald Trump to control the spread of virus. In India, no one can say that the government did not try its best.

While the economic destruction caused by the lockdown cannot be contested, it is also true that since this was a man-made crisis, the opening of the economy would automatically bring about the so-called revival. The word is a misnomer as the revival seen is just a scaled movement back to the normal path. However, the projection of this movement as a revival with discussions being on whether it was V-shaped or K-shaped drove home the point that the country was up and about. It was surprising that several analysts and economists as well as official spokespersons have taken it upon themselves to constantly project the great recovery in the economy thus conveying an impression that everything is just normal. Incessantly, creating the right sounds helps to make people forget the past as the promise of a better future is considered to be a good compensation.

As the majority form views and opinions based on what they read and hear and see in the media, this works. It obfuscates the true reality of the negative impact of the lockdown. By focusing on economic jargon the view conveyed is that everything is back on track which is not the case when one looks at the economic atrophy that took place in this period.

The fact is that economic growth for the year was going to be negative. It was also true that sequential opening of the economy would see the level of negativity improving. But it has been projected as being a major transformation which probably would be an exaggeration. We should not get overwhelmed by these numbers as the situation even before the lockdown was announced was grim with the economy slipping to growth of just 4.0% in FY20 of which only a part can be attributed to the last week effect. The last financial year was one with a normal monsoon and the expected demand drive did not materialize. The malaise of low job creation and declining investment rate was a part of the larger problem which has to be addressed with a new zeal.

Interestingly, 2021 or FY22 would be a statistical delight for all countries in the world as the movement from a negative growth number to a high and possibly double-digit range would resound well with the economists. There are already premature forecasts being made on whether it would be 9% or 12% or 15%. Forecasters have been bold and joined the ring as they can always be revised. Even this year there have been at least five revisions made by every forecasting agency depending on how the lockdown and unlock process went. The RBI was conservative to begin with and then threw its hat in the ring with –9.5% to scale it up to –7.5%. This upward movement in the negative number has been based on the fact that 'recovery is better than expected'.

To put in a perspective, India's GDP was ₹ 145.6 lakh crore in FY20. This has come down to ₹ 135.1 lakh crore in FY21. A 10% increase in FY22, which has been projected a V-shaped recovery will bring GDP value to ₹ 148.6 lakh crore, which is just 2.0% higher than FY20. FY20 was also derailed by the last week of lockdown with growth coming at just 4.0% with the level at ₹ 140.0 lakh crore in FY19. Therefore, caution should be exercised when interpreting economic numbers.

It is said that the one thing about economies' recovery is that it is uncertain. However so far, the kind of crises that we have had have been in the financial sector which spread to the real sectors. This particular crisis is different as it was manmade and started in the real sector. The crisis was different in so far that it was engendered by closing the tap and then opening it gradually at differential paces across geographies. This is why going by how the IMF has projected growth for 2020, there have been upward revisions for most countries.

There will be a lot of adjustments to be made by the people everywhere in the world. The hunt for the vaccine has taken almost a year and making it universal in terms of covering the entire population will take time. Setting timelines is very difficult. The success of the vaccine is still unknown and while clinical trials showed success to enable the embarking on a mass vaccination programme, the efficacy can be tested only with time. Will there be a repetition of lockdowns in if things do not work out? The answer is probably no. The omicron variant has raised apprehension again.

While as of December free movement of people across countries is banned with selective bubble arrangements being made bilaterally between countries, the progress of the vaccine and its effectiveness will hold the clue to the way countries open up to one another. Internally, it will be realized that the support provided by countries through stimuli is not something that can be done for a long period of time. The one-time stroke was necessary but continuing with fiscal stimuli looks unlikely. It can be argued that central banks have continued with QE for over a decade now, and hence a similar thing can be done with fiscal support. The cost is high for sure and will be a tough call to take. More likely the future response will be through the medical route rather than direct support such as cash payouts.

A lesson hopefully learnt is that there will be greater focus on healthcare in the coming years and both the Central and State Governments will invest on research and building capabilities in various areas to ensure that the nation is better prepared. In fact, while the number of infections in India was much lower than those in the USA and also resulted in a lower number of deaths, the access provided to infected patients by the medical infrastructure was commendable with the temporary structures being erected in the metro cities to accommodate the patients. This needs to be scaled up substantially in the country as there is a tendency to put these issues in the background once the crisis passes.

Governments in fact are bound to hit back at the taxpayers once then dust settles through various kinds of covid taxes. This cannot be avoided as they would have to recoup the expenses. This is inescapable. There is unlikely to be too much protest on this as it will be taken as a necessary cost and the middle class can look for challenging times.

It is said that epidemics which can turn pandemic cannot be ruled out in future and the covid rampage is the first of its kind. Countries must be geared up to recognizing such epidemics in advance and focusing on the laboratory to find cures as well as vaccinate the population. Clearly, the amount that has to be set aside will be enormous across the world but will be necessary. Also, a clear strategy has to be in hand to respond to such situations. Each epidemic will be unique, spread by different organisms for sure which will never be known in advance. But having contingency plans in place will be necessary. This has to be taken at the global level with cooperation being the focus. Just like how there is the WTO which has however been unsuccessful in fostering free trade, there needs to be organizations which get countries to cooperate and share expertise regularly to build foundations for tackling future events which will no longer be black swan ones. If this can be done, it will be success for the world.

Have Lessons been Learnt?

Here one has to blow hot and cold. The second wave of the pandemic hit us in late March 2021 and as usual we took a long time to recognize the same. Maharashtra was more alert as it was the first state to be affected. A lockdown followed while other states lived in denial until their population got infected. Amidst this second round of contagion, our politicians did not give up on campaigning in the states that were going for their Assembly Elections. This combination of carelessness and absence of character typified all parties and hence it is the political class which contributed to the second wave spreading from May onwards. The same people who welcomed crowds at rallies used the iron hand to curb movement once the results were out and the new government was formed. At this time too the Kumbh Mela was called off when some of the pious men caught the infection. Therefore, the nature of our reaction was unchanged from the first wave.

On the positive side, the lockdowns were less stressful as they were regional. Different interpretation of words like 'essential goods' created confusion across states. As the centre played no role, the airlines and railways were operational all through the period. Attention was diverted by the high number of cases and deaths which took place in the second wave. Hence, the human impact was more severe, though the economic impact less stressful. Probably, the discovery of a vaccine which was being administered with alacrity by the government provided hope for the people and notwithstanding the administrative issues, the performance of the centre has been remarkable here in terms of distributing the vaccines given the size of the population.

Chapter 20
Your Judgment

The book has tried to quite dispassionately put across the picture that emerged following the economic lockdown that was announced in March 2020. It came as a bolt from the blue though some may have been expecting it given that there were such instances of people being forced to stay indoors in countries like Italy. However, in our case there were just a few cases of infection and while the single day curfew did send signals that something big was coming, it was a shocker considering that no authority quite knew what it meant in the sense that it was not clear as to how the lockdown had to be interpreted which gave rise to a lot of subjectivity. Governance can never be subjective because it leads to anomalies in terms of action and repercussions. This is what happened.

All the issues have been placed threadbare in this book and views been given as far as possible from the economic standpoint because numbers tell all. The arguments and conclusions are free from emotion as they would tend to sway the reader. After all that has happened can we really say we did the right thing with the collateral damage being the cost? Or can we say that it was another blunder that caused pain and no real gain as we had to retract when it went out of control? The answer will be different from the point of view of how the reader interprets the fallout.

Here the two viewpoints are placed in fairly straight forward terms supporting the decision to have a lockdown as well as arguments that prove it was another economic blunder. You may choose which way makes sense, or if unsure, agree to both sides without taking a stance. It surely is a difficult decision to take, and this is a conundrum faced by every country which faced the pandemic and looked across borders to see what others did and tried to do better. The second wave tended to put similar pressure on governments especially in Europe.

The Arguments in Favour of the Lockdown

The Indian Government decided to go in for the lockdown on 24th March for 21 days. It was largely believed that if there was no human interaction, there would-be fewer chances of spread of the virus. While this was a very bold assumption to be made, the fact that a start was made was commendable. As the infection was supposed to last for 14 days anyone who was infected would get revealed in this period and hence after 21 days the country would be generally safe with all carriers being identified. As this was too simplistic a course and the country was too large with multitudes of people who could not be checked, there were extensions of this lockdown on April 14th, May 1st and May 17th till May end. On May 30th, it was announced that the restrictions would be lifted and from 8th June onwards the unlock process started. On May 30th, there were approximately 180,000 cases and on June 30th was 585,000. On June 16th, the number crossed one million. August 6th witnessed the two million mark and September 15th witnessed the five million mark. On December 18th, the 10 million mark was passed.

The arguments for having a lockdown were broadly the following.

- A decision had to be taken and there was not much time to think. Therefore, it had to be done immediately and there was no time for planning. Unlike demonetization which was a crisis where the pros and cons could have been studied in advance as it was not bound by a time frame, in case of a possible pandemic there was little time to study the details.
- Other countries had done such lockdowns of different varieties and hence what was done by India was not unique.

- Following from what other countries had done, one had to act fast, and there was no reason not to pursue such an approach.
- Given the size of population and high density, it had to be more severe than in other countries and hence was in order.
- There was regular communication by the Centre with the PM speaking periodically talking about what could and what could not be done. It was a different issue that federalism in the country empowers states to take their set of decisions which can be different from that of the Centre.
- The government was proactive to the developments that were taking place and hence while the issue of migrants was a scar on the process followed, there was nothing better that could be done. On the governemnt's part accommodation and food was provided at shelters. As conditions improved arrangements were made to ferry migrants back to their homes by the special trains that were deployed for this purpose. Given the logistics involved this had to take time and the government worked hard all through to expedite the process.
- Relief through free food was provided by the government to ensure that the poor were not left out.
- The PM had repeatedly told companies to not lay off workers and to pay the salaries. Besides suasion, the government could do no better in a democracy.
- The RBI came in to provide funds at a low cost to borrowers after providing a moratorium and hence there was enough done on the credit side for enterprise.
- The government through its series of reforms spread over seven months fine-tuned policies to ensure that there was return to the path of normalcy. Reforms announced were to work in the short and medium runs and hence were comprehensive. All vulnerable sectors were targeted including street vendors to ensure that they could come back to the mainstream.

- While the stimulus was not from the budget the volume of impact was around ₹ 30 lakh crore which was 15% of GDP. This was more comprehensive than just giving cash as it embedded several reforms too and worked with the market forces. Thus, the government became a very active enabler of reforms rather than an entity which just transfered funds. Giving free money was done where it was needed the most which is to the poor through cash transfers and food. There are limits to which one can give doles to everyone.
- The unlock process was invoked quite early notwithstanding the pressures that were there of the infection cases increasing. It was a pragmatic view to be taken and was done in a calibrated manner. This had to be done to protect the economy as the spread of infection and the economic revival plan were delinked. The calibration ensured that activity was back on stream and the industries which had more social interaction were given lower priority, i.e. services in terms of unlocking.
- The States were advised not to have lockdowns without taking permission from the Centre. This was the most that the Centre could do to ensure there were no future lockdowns.
- There was strategic intervention only when required when it came to stopping activity as was the case with the temporary ban on flights from England in December following news of the outbreak of a new strain of the virus.

Therefore, the entire approach of the government was quite well framed with bans coming in the beginning; and then the unlocking started quite early in June keeping in mind the sensitivities involved. There was surely collateral damage like jobs being lost, output falling, certain industries being under threat of extinction, migrants facing an uncertain future, etc. But these are costs of any disaster and this was a once in a lifetime shock for which there were no available templates. It happens when there is a war or a natural disaster of wide proportions and this analogy holds here too though admittedly the decision taken was by the government.

The Counter Argument

The counter argument narrative may now be presented here which shows that there were a lot of missed chances and the pain caused was one sided for which there has been no compensation.

- The declaration of a lockdown should have been done after carefully planning the approach so that the outcomes were less harmful. We had the time in March when there were very few cases.
- The Wuhan story was known from November 2019 and while the spread was to Europe to begin with the various think tanks of the country should have started having a plan in place for the possible spread to India. There were isolated cases reported even by January 2020 and there should have logically been a plan in place. It did reflect lack of alertness on the part of the think tanks.
- As mentioned at the beginning, the imposition was at a time when there was limited infection and with limited restrictions could have taken a month to devise a lockdown programme.
- The people who go most affected were the poor which is always the case when it comes to any calamity. There can be no excuse for treating them in a high-handed manner in a democratic nation as some of the images presented were reminiscent of the post partition times.
- The damage done to the SME segment was immense. They had already gone down under post demonetization and GST was a second blow. By stopping activity these enterprises had slim chances of revival as they had to perforce relieve employees as their business came to an end. As they operate on tight financial lines, liquidation was a possibility.
- Treating the migrants like unwanted people was unpardonable. How can a government let 10-20 million people walk to their hometowns bearing the

stick of police and hunger for days with no support? This situation was probably worse than the status of refugees during partition where there was a background of separation. In this case, the state cannot be absolved of such treatment. Even if they could not be supported, physically assaulting citizens who had to go back to their hometowns because of displacement reflects failure of administration.

- The free food package given was not adequate as people without an income cannot live on just cereals and pulses. Besides those with no ration cards could not draw the supplies and getting through the red tape was a challenge. The scheme was just tokenism which helped at the periphery without touching the core—absence of sustainable income.
- The Atma Nirbhar programme was more of a series of reforms which were not targeted at the current problem. While credit guarantees, free food, cash transfers were direct measures which helped, most of the ₹ 30 lakh crore was more in the form of indirect measures through the credit channels which cannot be called a stimulus. RBI giving TLTROs is not really a stimulus. Further, allowing employees to draw on their own salary and allowances in advance is not a stimulus. The package was inadequate and did not address the real problem and talking of future reforms in a situation of grave economic crisis made little sense and obfuscated attention.
- In this context, we need to compare what other governments did which was in the realm of direct tax cuts and transfers to all. This was not done in India and hence lacked punch.
- The unlock process was more due to the government realizing that their income in the form of tax revenue got impacted when the economy collapsed and hence that led to a very gradual opening of the economy. One did get a sense that it was invoked only when it was

realized that the government got affected the most when revenues slipped sharply, and it was hard to carry on the administration. Even here the calibrated measures looked more hesitant than real.

- There have been absolutely no tax breaks given to anyone. The only concession was deferment of TDS which had to be paid anyway. The deal could have been better.
- All schemes which were announced ended by November and hence there was no extension of any benefit as such.
- No relief given to people who lost jobs or had to take salary cuts. This affects the overall spending power of the country besides the morale of those who were out of work.
- As various economic indicators show there was a fall in industrial production, erasing of income in sectors such as entertainment, hotels, restaurants, airlines, tourism, etc., GDP growth, exports, infrastructure investment delayed and so on. In the first three months, the supply chains were disrupted quite sharply due to the restrictions placed on movement of goods. These are the pure economic costs that cannot be contested.

The point here is that while a recovery will take place for sure as no economy ever goes down forever, is there any accountability for such economic destruction? Was there an apology coming from anywhere for imposing such a harsh punishment on people? Or is it a case of believing that every catastrophe has certain damage inflicted and it is the way of the world? In case of a war or a cyclone which are natural disasters there is no blame on anyone and at best one can ask if the administration had taken steps to provide relief or warn the people. In this case, there can be no such excuse considering that the lockdown did not help to stop the spread of the virus and it was a human decision.

The reader can take her/his call on this entire framework of lockdown as there are strong arguments on both sides. As has been said in the beginning, the proponents of the lockdown have argued that if it were not done, the spread would have been higher. The Economic Survey for 2020-21 has argued in detail as to how the lockdown was the best approach taken and the entire process was handled adeptly by the State.

But data does not support this line of thought as the number multiplied subsequently and the fact that they increased when the unlock had to take place suggests that locking people in was not viable. Besides, one will never know as such hypotheses can never be validated.

But the broader question is whether we have learnt our lessons. There is still no clear answer here as countries are reacting still by having selective lockdowns which is prevalent in India too. Night curfews and restrictions on movements have been a part of our system as late as December. The answers will never be known for sure as governments are still in the dark about the right action to be taken. Stopping movement between countries or states is at best a desperate move which works on hope rather than assured result. As governments cannot be seen to be doing nothing, they prefer such restrictive action.

Will governments respond in a similar manner if there are more of such pandemics? Will they struggle to find the balance between combating such a disease and keeping the economic wheels moving? It is clear that government support cannot be forever as there are limits to what can be done. The Western nations did better because their first wave came to an end faster than in our case where the tapering off started more post December. This is something that governments all over have to ruminate over and have a policy framework in place that works like a template for future action. That is the only way out.

We reacted differently in April 2021, but only slightly. Lockdowns was the solution but it became regional. But this time there was little help coming as the centre continued to pledge only free foodgrains. But states sat back and let nature take it course.

References

As a lot of information that has been quoted in this book is from various web sites, the same references have been provided here.

1. https://www.thehindubusinessline.com/companies/auto-component-industry-facing-rs-1000-1200-crore-production-loss-each-day-acma/article31197123.ece
2. https://www.telegraphindia.com/business/coronavirus-lockdown-durables-fear-30-sales-drop/cid/1770096
3. https://cse.azimpremjiuniversity.edu.in/wp-content/uploads/2020/06/Compilation-of-findings-APU-COVID-19-Livelihoods-Survey_Final.pdf
4. https://www.financialexpress.com/economy/retail-trade-suffers-rs-15-5-lakh-crore-business-loss-due-to-covid-cait/2028914/
5. https://www.financialexpress.com/industry/covid-19-pandemic-impact-majority-of-hotel-operators-expect-up-to-2-years-for-revenue-recovery-says-jll-survey/2009877/
6. https://www.businesstoday.in/current/economy-politics/hotels-report-82-drop-in-occupancy-recovery-unlikely-before-september/story/405355.html
7. https://economictimes.indiatimes.com/industry/services/hotels-/-restaurants/total-room-inventory-occupancy-for-hotels-in-india-stood-at-29-in-2020-str/articleshow/80451528.cms
8. https://economictimes.indiatimes.com/small-biz/startups/newsbuzz/about-70-per-cent-startups-impacted-by-covid-19-survey/articleshow/76801147.cms?from=mdr
9. http://www.ficci.in/SEDocument/20523/FICCI_Economic_Outlook_Survey-July2020.pdf
10. https://retail.economictimes.indiatimes.com/news/food-entertainment/food-services/cafe-coffee-day-shuts-280-more-outlets-in-april-june-quarter-citing-profitability-issues/77063201

11. https://www.freepressjournal.in/mumbai/mumbai-real-estate-island-city-sees-drop-in-sales-sold-204-units-in-q1-of-2020-21-says-report
12. https://www.csds.in/covid_19_rural_survey_findings_2020
13. https://www.newindianexpress.com/nation/2020/jun/20/communities-remain-hungry-amid-lockdown-migrant-workers-worst-hit-study-2159094.html
14. https://www.telegraphindia.com/india/lockdown-impact-continues-to-affect-migrants/cid/1794271
15. https://www.worldbank.org/en/news/press-release/2020/10/07/covid-19-to-add-as-many-as-150-million-extreme-poor-by-2021
16. https://www.businessinsider.in/retail/news/from-shoppers-stop-and-raymond-to-small-retailers-thousands-of-people-have-lost-their-jobs/articleshow/76354403.cms
17. https://www.newindianexpress.com/business/2020/apr/30/reliance-cuts-employees-salary-by-10-to-50-per-cent-ambani-to-forgo-entire-salary-2137433.html
18. https://www.reuters.com/article/us-health-coronavirus-oyo-idUSKCN2240XD
19. https://theprint.in/india/governance/to-cut-costs-indian-railways-to-axe-thousands-of-retired-staff-it-had-re-hired/440058/
20. https://www.thenewsminute.com/article/pay-cuts-india-media-continue-ndtv-toi-hindu-ht-cut-pay-due-covid-19-123390
21. https://www.newslaundry.com/2020/04/16/hindustan-times-cuts-take-home-pay-of-staff-offers-insurance-cover-for-their-kin
22. https://timesofindia.indiatimes.com/business/india-business/pandemic-impact-indigo-to-lay-off-10-employees/articleshow/77068489.cms
23. https://www.ilo.org/asia/publications/WCMS_753369/lang--en/index.htm
24. https://www.cmie.com/kommon/bin/sr.php?kall=warticle&dt=2020-09-14%2021:47:53&msec=416
25. https://www.livemint.com/news/india/one-out-of-every-five-in-informal-sector-are-out-of-work-during-oct-dec-survey-11611761332012.html

Index

A

Airlines, 40, 50, 62

Automobiles, 45, 172

Aviation, 62, 118, 175

Azim Premji University, 10, 64

B

Budget, 95, 98, 100, 102, 125, 134, 152, 161

C

Capex, 100

Cash transfers, 94

Centre, 8, 15, 23, 28, 31, 38, 39, 40, 45, 56, 96, 97, 98, 100, 105, 106, 107, 119, 124, 127, 139, 147, 179, 180, 181, 188, 189

Compensation cess, 104

Construction, 26, 27, 49, 52, 55, 78

Consumption, 53, 55

CPI, 85, 88

Credit, 72, 74, 113, 115, 117, 121, 132, 133, 153, 162

Customs, 98, 101

D

Diwali, 35, 40, 52, 56, 66, 124, 126

E

ECLGS, 72, 75, 153, 154, 156

Elections, 180, 181, 184

Electricity, 49, 52, 55, 78

Employment, 126, 137

Entertainment, 174

EPF, 114, 120

F

Farmers, 48

FICCI, 12, 13, 14, 194

FMCG, 59, 92

FRBM, 100, 106, 107

G

GDP, 20, 45, 47, 48, 49, 50, 52, 53, 54, 55, 56, 68, 79, 80, 95, 100, 101, 126, 129, 130, 131, 133, 134, 135, 136, 137, 138, 139, 182, 189, 192

GeM, 69

GST, 23, 56, 68, 69, 72, 73, 97, 100, 101, 103, 104, 105, 106, 107, 124, 161, 190

H

Hospitality, 12, 13, 170

I

IMF, 47, 53, 129, 130, 138, 139, 183

Indian Railways, 23, 60

Inflation, 84, 88

Investment, 53, 55, 56, 76, 77, 115

J

Jan Dhan, 11

K

Kamath Committee, 75, 155

L

Layoffs, 64

Liquidity, 115, 120, 137, 140, 141

Loan, 112, 132

M

Make in India, 112

Manufacturing, 14, 49, 52, 55, 126, 178

MGNREGA, 18, 24, 25, 26

Migrants, 17, 23, 33, 116

Mining, 48, 52, 55, 118

Moratorium, 147, 152

MPC, 88, 140, 141, 142

MSME, 68, 69, 70, 71, 72, 113, 114, 120, 150

N

NABARD, 117, 121, 122, 142, 162

NBFC, 73, 115, 120, 150

P

PLI, 126

PMI, 80, 81, 82, 111

Prices, 55, 87

R

Railways, 23, 40, 51, 60

Ration card, 119

RBI, 47, 69, 71, 72, 73, 74, 78, 92, 94, 95, 98, 99, 100, 107, 115, 121, 122, 123, 126, 127, 135, 140, 141, 142, 143, 144, 146, 147, 150, 151, 152, 155, 156, 159, 160, 161, 163, 182, 188, 191

Real estate, 46, 51

Reforms, 188

Revenue, 12, 101, 120

S

Salary bill, 65

Section, 144, 4, 6

Services, 26, 67, 97, 114

SMEs, 19, 26, 31, 59, 68, 69, 70, 71, 72, 74, 75, 112, 121, 122, 123, 132, 134, 135, 136, 137, 146, 149, 151, 153, 154, 156, 157, 159, 162

SOP, 40

Start-ups, 13

States, 3, 8, 10, 12, 22, 23, 24, 25, 26, 27, 28, 29, 30, 31, 33, 36, 37, 38, 39, 40, 41, 45, 48, 50, 56, 60, 71, 97, 98, 100, 106, 107, 116, 119, 124, 125, 138, 139, 147, 162, 179, 180, 189

Stimulus, 111

T

TLTRO, 141, 142, 143, 145

Trade, 52, 55, 132, 133

Transport, 78, 86, 87, 175

U

Unlock, 11, 31, 38

V

Vande Bharat Mission, 12

W

WMA, 98, 100